D1532430

FOOTBALL'S
LAST IRON MEN

1934, Yale vs. Princeton,
and One Stunning Upset

NORMAN L. MACHT

University of Nebraska Press | Lincoln & London

All photographs courtesy of Yale University
Athletic Department Archives.

Library of Congress Cataloging-in-
Publication Data

Macht, Norman L. (Norman Lee), 1929–
Football's last iron men : 1934, Yale vs.
Princeton, and one stunning upset / by
Norman L. Macht.
    p. cm.
ISBN 978-0-8032-3401-7 (pbk. : alk. paper)
1. Yale University—Football—History.
2. Princeton University—Football—History.
3. Sports rivalries—United States. I. Title.
GV958.Y3M33   2010
796.332'64097409043—dc22
2009050412

Set in Swift EF by Kim Essman.

CONTENTS

ILLUSTRATIONS

Following p. 72

ACKNOWLEDGMENTS

The basics of college football today are the same as they were seventy-seven years ago: running, passing, kicking, blocking, and tackling.

In other ways, the game is significantly different. In 1934 every man played both offense and defense. Substitutions were limited. Sixty-minute men were common. Students weighing 160 or 170 pounds, clad in thinly padded uniforms and pliable leather helmets, played for the fun and glory, not the NFL scouts. The game belonged to the men on the field. Quarterbacks called all their own plays with no help from the sidelines.

That's the way it was when Yale and Princeton met in the most unforgettable battle in one of college football's oldest rivalries. The threads that came together on that warm November afternoon in 1934 began as long as a dozen years earlier.

To tell their stories in their own words, the author had the pleasure and privilege of visiting nine of the Yale starters: Bob Train, Clare Curtin, Ben Grosscup, Stan Fuller, Larry Kelley, Kim Whitehead, Jimmy DeAngelis, Meredith Scott, and Jerry Roscoe. I also visited assistant business manager Lou Walker and scout Bob Hall and corresponded with second-string end John Hersey.

Princetonians interviewed included Gil Lea, Ben Delaney, Hugh MacMillan, and the widow of Pepper Constable.

Other sources included several New York newspapers, the *Chicago Tribune*, *New Haven Register*, *Trenton Evening Times*, Yale and Princeton athletic department archives, student newspapers, and alumni publications.

Thanks to football historian Jim Campbell for his assistance and to Ed Edmonds and George Rugg for their research at the Joyce Sports Research Collection at the Hesburgh Libraries of the University of Notre Dame.

Introduction

FOR THE FIRST TIME SINCE WALL STREET LAID AN EGG IN 1929, Palmer Stadium in Princeton would be filled for the Yale-Princeton game on Saturday, November 17, 1934. Standing room behind the end zones would raise the capacity to fifty-three thousand. The popular one-dollar end-zone seats had long been sold out. Students were deluged with telegrams from dads: "Get four good tickets to Yale game." The rumored scalpers' price in New York was $25 for the $3.50 reserved and $2.20 general admission. The split of the gate receipts would give both schools their biggest payday of the year: $79,370.

The worst of the Depression seemed to be behind the nation. For the first time in five years, the economy had grown. Industrial production was up 10 percent. Aided by the alphabet soup of New Deal programs, unemployment had fallen from near 25 percent to under 15. More families could now afford an occasional standing rib roast at twenty-one cents a pound. After a three-year slide, the stock market was in the middle of a bull run that had begun in mid-1933.

Railroad workers had been busy for two days erecting signs to direct the special trains from Philadelphia, New York, and New Haven. Specials from New York left every few minutes from Penn Station between 9 a.m. and 12:15 p.m.; the round-trip fare was $1.50. The New Haven Railroad scheduled a special train of parlor cars, coaches, and dining cars leaving New Haven at 8:55 a.m., arriving at 12:15 p.m., and departing shortly after the game for $6.95 round trip. Luncheon was $1, and a special dinner on the way home was $1.25. By noon the siding adjacent to the campus would resemble the switching yards in Chicago.

Additional state troopers had been arriving since Friday to

handle the anticipated traffic. A network of ropes stretched across parking fields to control the thousands of automobiles.

Among the Ivy colleges, the weekend of a home game against a traditional rival was the social event of the fall season. For the young ladies of the Seven Sisters universities, an invitation to a football weekend elevated their social status among envious friends and roommates. It also set off a week of dizzying preparation: what to wear, which hairstyle to choose, how to deal with nervous, inexperienced (or smooth, experienced) beaus and boyfriends. Untold numbers of virgins would be undone and marriages proposed—some accepted, some rejected, some forgotten or regretted in the morning.

The game itself was of little importance; all the girls needed to know was when to cheer. Their anticipation centered on the fraternity parties, the black-tie proms, the overnight stays at volunteer chaperones' homes (there were no sororities on the all-male campuses), the tell-all sharing of intimate details of their adventures on their return to Wellesley or Smith or Vassar or wherever on Sunday.

They were up before dawn Saturday to catch trains that would take them to Princeton Junction by noon. Then there was a short ride on the two-car "Toonerville Trolley," which ran between the station and the school's railyard—twelve minutes to rearrange bouncing hairdos, repair makeup, rehearse smiles for the boys they hoped would be waiting to greet them.

Typical November weather—light snow and cold, fifty-mile-an-hour winds—had forced both teams indoors for practice during the week. But Saturday dawned unusually clear and warm. This was not the November Thomas Hood had in mind when he wrote these lines:

No sun—no moon!
No morn—no noon—

No dawn—no dusk—no proper time of day.
No warmth, no cheerfulness, no healthful ease,
No comfortable feel in any member—
No shade, no shine, no butterflies, no bees,
No fruits, no flowers, no leaves, no birds!—
November!

By noon the temperature was climbing into the sixties.

The Yale first-stringers and jayvees had departed New Haven at 10 a.m. Friday for the 130-mile ride to Princeton. While the jayvees handed the Princeton jayvees their first defeat, 6-0, at University Field, the varsity went through a light workout at Palmer. They spent the night at the Stacy-Trenton Hotel in Trenton.

Princeton head coach Fritz Crisler took his team six miles away to Lawrenceville Prep School to get away from the Friday night rallies and social ramble.

Princeton was riding a 15-game unbeaten streak extending over two years and three days. Yale was 3-3 and at least a 2-to-1 underdog. But that didn't matter. This was Yale-Princeton, a rivalry begun in 1873 and since 1876 interrupted only in 1917–18, when both schools had cancelled their college schedules. No alcohol was allowed in Palmer, unlike at the flowing Bowl of Yale. No rules are 100 percent enforceable, but the noise and excitement of this day would not have to be augmented by hip flasks.

The festive atmosphere was reminiscent of better times. There was noise and laughter and men and women decked out in their finest autumn outfits. Early arrivals provided an unaccustomed large crowd of spectators at a freshman soccer game between the two schools, won by Princeton, 4-2. The aroma of grilled hot dogs and hamburgers filled the air. The lawns were filled with picnic basket parties, the equivalent of today's tailgate parties. A pair of undergrads were stopped when they tried to smuggle eleven cats dyed orange into the stadium and turn them loose.

An hour before the 2:00 p.m. kickoff, an unbroken stream of ticket holders began filling the concrete stadium. They didn't know that they were about to witness a feat that would never again be seen on a major college football field.

1 | In the Beginning

THE EMBRYO THAT GREW TO BECOME AMERICAN COLLEGIATE football was conceived on November 6, 1869, in New Brunswick, New Jersey. Its parents were Princeton and Rutgers. It bore little resemblance to its later mature form. The birth was reported in a brief back-page squib in the *New York Tribune* two days later: "Twenty-five of the students of Rutgers College played the same number of Princeton College a game of foot-ball on Saturday. After an exciting contest of one hour the Rutgers were declared the winners, the score standing 6 [goals] to 4."

The rules had been drawn up by Princeton captain William S. Gummers. The ball could not be carried or passed. It could be advanced only by kicking or batting it with the hand or head or body. No tripping or holding, no tackling or collaring was allowed.

More than anything else, the game resembled two human walls colliding. The players wore no helmets or special uniforms. There were literally no holds barred once they were all down in a heap.

Other East Coast schools began experimenting with the game. In 1872 a group of Yale students invited a team from Columbia with two years' experience to come to New Haven on November 16. The account of Yale's first football game was given prominent display on the front page of the *New York Times* the next day. It's worth reproducing almost in full because it's the best description available of an early game, and it seems to mark a genetic trail for Yale football two generations later. The game still resembled soccer more than today's football. There were fourteen men on a side. About four hundred persons, mostly students, were present.

The match game of foot-ball, which Yale challenged Columbia to play, came off this afternoon at Hamilton Park. The Columbia men arrived, some of them on this morning's boat, and some of them on the eleven o'clock train. They were a splendid-looking set of men, in good spirits, and so confident of winning that their backers bet on them freely and even offered odds as great as five to two. The game was to be played with a rubber ball, best five goals out of nine, and in case of darkness coming on, the side ahead at that time was to be declared the winner. Game was to be called at 2 1/2 [2:30] p.m., but with the usual unavoidable delay, it did not really begin until about 2 3/4 [2:45]. As the men stood at their positions before the ball was canted for the first time, the difference between them was very noticeable. Columbia's champions were large, heavy, and solid, while the Yale men were small and seemed chosen more for activity and speed. They were, too, differently arranged. Columbia had two men near the goal posts, and the others were scattered carelessly about the field, but the Yale men were placed with almost mathematical precision. At the goal posts were the two "keepers," and on their right and left two side men. At a considerable distance from and in front of the goal were the middle-men, eight in number, and arranged like a crescent, with its horns resting on either side of the field. In the centre of the crescent were the six "rushers," who were to follow the ball wherever it went, and who, as they were to do the hard fighting, were the heaviest men on the Yale side. Two "pea-nutters," who were to keep ahead of the ball and when it came near the goal to drive it over, completed the number. To look at the men and the disposition of them, it seemed as though Columbia would play the hardest and most energetic game, and that if Yale beat it could only be by force of strategy. Platt opened the game for Yale by a rousing cant which carried it over half the field. Then the Columbia men got it, and with a rush carried it ahead, and on, until it seemed as though by force of weight and numbers they would carry it straight through the goal. And they did get it clear up to the posts, but here one of the keepers made a very pretty stop and sent it to one of the middle-men. He passed it to a second and he to a third, who kicked it, not down but across the field where stood another ready to receive it and carry it still further.

"All was done so quietly that before the Columbia men really perceived it, the ball had been kicked not through, but around them, and the goal was won by Yale in fifteen minutes."

Yale scored two more goals before darkness fell for a 3–0 victory.

Yale and Princeton met for the first time the following year. A few years later the following unsigned account of that game appeared in an athletic history of Princeton:

At last arrangements were completed for the Yale game. The Princeton men had been training by running a half hour a day in the gym and by frequent practice in kicking. On November 14 the twenty Princetonians went to New Haven on the night boat and nearly froze. The next day at two o'clock they were on the field ready to play the first football game between Yale and Princeton. Yale won the toss and gave Princeton the ball which Moffet bucked [ran into the line] and the game started.

During the first half Princeton was roughly handled. Yale played a bucking, rushing game which years later was developed into interference. This surprised and confused the visitors whose policy was to follow the ball closely and neglect their Yale opponents. Yale probably would have won, but luckily two men tried to kick the ball at the same time. Each toe hit it squarely and the ball burst. It was fully a half hour before another could be secured, and during this delay Princetonians gathered together and decided to try the rushing game. With this added time to talk it over, they came back to outcharge Yale, scoring the winning points before dark.

(In January 1934 the remains of the ball, which had been stuffed, not inflated, were donated to Princeton by George M. Gumm, the Yale man of the pair who had kicked it. "We kicked it at the same time," Gumm recalled, "and the ball rose into the air about twenty feet and fell with the stuffing kicked out of it.")

After a lapse of two years, the two schools again began their annual meetings. By 1880 the number of players on each side had settled to eleven. They wore canvas shirts laced up the front and canvas knickers. Thin leather helmets began to appear.

The University of Chicago was among the first to use football to publicize and promote the school. President William Rainey Harper hired Yale star Amos Alonzo Stagg to field a team that would bring recognition to the new campus in 1892. Stagg succeeded. After his first year he had seventeen consecutive winning seasons. In 1894 the Chicagoans traveled to California and played a pair of games against Stanford. They played nineteen games that year, winning eleven. Stagg remained for forty years, compiling a .671 winning percentage.

Football was dominated by the old-line colleges of the East until the 1920s, when Chicago and Princeton split two games, and Knute Rockne brought his midwestern heroes from Notre Dame to New York to play Army. During that good-times decade crowds of eighty thousand were not uncommon in stadiums like the Yale Bowl. Newspapers devoted gridiron-sized space to the sport each week. In 1923, when Yale routed Princeton, 27–0, the *New York Times* gave it enough ink to print the collected works of Charles Dickens.

Big games produced big payoffs for the participants. Fielding a winning team was seen as a way to bankroll all the money-losing teams in the athletic department and to coax more generous contributions from alumni, which gave them (or empowered them to exercise) a louder voice in the hiring and firing of coaches and recruiting of star high school and prep school players. The use of financial and other inducements became widespread. Yale fullback Stan Fuller said that in 1929 he was offered a free ride at Ohio State and alumni would see that he had spending money. If you couldn't make the grade academically, colleges would pay your way at a prep school until you met the entrance requirements. It was said that Columbia, for example, was subsidizing athletes in every prep school in the Northeast. Professional coaches were fast replacing schools' former football heroes or other alumni coaching in part-time, sometimes volunteer, capacities. The athletic tail began to wag the academic body.

In 1929 the Carnegie Foundation blasted the subsidizing and recruiting of athletes.

The financial fountain ran dry—temporarily—with the Depression. Crowds dwindled. At some schools athletic receipts fell by half from the palmy days of 1927–28. Schedules were cut back, ticket prices reduced. Some sports were eliminated. In 1932 the new president of Washington & Jefferson recommended abandoning big-time football, which was now costing the school $40,000 a year in free tuition, room and board, and books for the student athletes. But the financial problems of most universities also had the effect of increasing the pressure to field winning teams.

The Carnegie report had divided the colleges into three groups: those who went into the open market and bid high for talent; those who used more subtle inducements while maintaining a facade of dignity; and those who rejected recruiting inducements and risked mediocre teams and declining gate receipts.

Harvard, Yale, and Princeton were in the last category. In turning down petitions from undergrads to approve postseason games like the Rose Bowl, the Princeton Athletic Association cited its agreement with Yale to ban such appearances and explained its position: "Back of this principle is a definite philosophy of the administration of college sports. This philosophy is based on the premise that athletics, if properly conducted, are an integral part of a well-rounded college training. They are beneficial as long as they occupy a normal and natural place in the whole college educational program. When they tend to usurp more than their rightful share of interest and attention, they become harmful and should be restricted."

The river of tradition still flowed through the ranks of some alumni. A letter from the class of 1913 backed up the administration: football was, after all, just a sport; no reason to overturn tradition. Playing old rivals each year ought to be enough excitement for anybody.

2 | The Rules

IN ORDER TO APPRECIATE THE EVENTS AND ACHIEVEMENTS described in this narrative, it is essential to understand the rules of football then in effect. Like baseball, the sport has changed little enough for someone sitting in Palmer Stadium in November 1934 to awaken after a seventy-five-year nap and still understand what was going on in the latest Super Bowl. It has also changed so much that a twenty-first-century fan, whisked back in time to that day in Princeton, would wonder why they did the things they did the way they did them.

The most striking thing a visitor from the future would notice is the lack of substitutes. Nobody seemed to leave the game, even when the ball changed hands. Actually a coach could send in an entirely new team at any time—and Fritz Crisler often did. But any players who came out could not go back in until the next quarter. (Until 1932 they couldn't go back in until the next half.) That slowed the in-and-out traffic considerably. It meant that a man had to be strong on both offense and defense just to make the team. Each player had strengths and weaknesses, but the specialist was unknown. If a team had no dependable kicker who could handle the other responsibilities of a back, it usually ran a play for the point after touchdown. Either way, it counted for only one point.

It was not unusual for one or two or even seven or eight men to play the entire sixty minutes. In 1926 Brown had played Yale and Dartmouth on successive Saturdays using only the same eleven men in both games.

A less visible but equally significant difference was this: the game belonged to the players. The quarterback called all the plays. He was the field commander. He could see the general staff sitting on the bench, but there could be no communication between them—no intercom, no sending in plays via messenger subs, no surreptitious nods or crossed arms or other signaling gestures, no conferring during a time-out. A violation drew a 5-yard penalty. In his first game as a coach at Yale, against Columbia, Greasy Neale suspected that the Lions' coach, Lou Little, was giving illegal signs from the bench through a coach wearing white gloves, but he couldn't prove it. Greasy Neale and Fritz Crisler could design all the trick plays they wanted, but it was up to the quarterback to decide when to use them. This put a tremendous burden on the quarterback and the coach who had to prepare him. It was Greasy Neale's responsibility at Yale, and we'll see how he carried it out.

A man taken out at the end of a quarter could not go back in until after one play had been run in the next quarter to avoid his being sent back in with instructions. No substitute at any time was allowed to speak until after one play had been run, and officials watched the players in the huddles. The penalty was 5 yards.

At about the same time that Babe Ruth began the revolution that changed baseball strategy from one base at a time to the circuit clout, the forward pass had begun to open up football from 3 yards and a cloud of dust to the spectacular aerial attack. As far back as 1920 Greasy Neale's Marietta College team had once completed nine consecutive passes in a game. The ball, which in its earliest unmeasured conception had resembled a pumpkin, had gradually become slimmer, like a dieting chorus girl, and was now down to 21 1/4 inches around the middle. This new weapon confused defenses and threatened to turn every game into the equivalent of baseball's slugfests. William "Pop" Corbin, a Yale hero of the old days, said the game had become more like basketball. College football's viewers with alarm had persuaded the rules committee to take steps to curb the "wild passing game." A rule was passed that made it a crime to throw more than one incomplete pass within a set of downs. The penalty was 5 yards for each offense. Even harsher, throwing an incomplete pass into the end zone resulted in a touchback. The defense got the ball on its own 20.

By 1934 Fritz Crisler was a member of the rules committee. The rule makers now believed that the defense had caught up with the offense, and they eased the passing restrictions. Eased, not eliminated. They revoked the 5-yard penalty that had been in effect for all incomplete passes after the first in a series of downs except in the end zone. The first incomplete pass thrown into the end zone no longer resulted in a touchback. But an incomplete pass in the end zone on fourth down still turned the ball over to the defense on its 20.

Yale head coach Ducky Pond agreed with Corbin. He thought the passing restrictions should be retained "to prevent teams from throwing passes wildly."

In any case, the passer had to be at least 5 yards behind the line of scrimmage.

The touchback rule was changed in 1934. If a kick receiver downed the ball or was tackled in the end zone, the ball came out to the 20. Previously it had been scored as a safety.

To placate the game's detractors and make it safer, new rules banned airborne blocks, flying tackles, and the flying wedge, a popular juggernaut for razing defenders on kickoff returns. The defense could no longer strike an opponent on the head, neck, or face. Defensive linemen could no longer use their hands except in a straight, stiff-arm position. The ball was dead if any part of the carrier other than the hands or feet touched the ground.

The goal posts had been moved back 10 yards behind the goal line for safety reasons. That would reduce the number of field goals. Fritz Crisler favored lowering the crossbar and widening the posts to encourage more field goal attempts. But it didn't happen.

Another change in 1934 turned the quick kick into a potent weapon that has since disappeared. Previously the ball had to be dropped and kicked before it touched the ground. This made it almost impossible to punt with any accuracy, and the play was seldom used. Now the kicker or another player could hold it until it was kicked. As it was explained to the coaches, a quarterback could fake a spinner into the line or a pass, for instance, and let the punter kick it right out of the quarterback's hands. If the punter took the snap directly from the center, he could now hold the ball until he kicked it.

All of these rule changes were gone over during pre-season blackboard sessions.

In 1934 the college game was still trying to maintain an aura of sportsmanship and fair play as a gentleman's game. At a session to explain the new rules, a coach asked, "Is the quarterback while calling signals permitted to change the tone of his voice, quicken it or slow up?" The answer: "It is left to the discretion of the officials to decide what the intent is. If it is intended to draw the defense offside, such action will be ruled illegal."

3 | Fritz Crisler

ON THE WAY TO BECOMING A DOCTOR, HERBERT ORIN CRISLER accidentally turned into a football coach.

Born on January 12, 1899, near the tiny town of Earlville, Illinois, eighty miles west of Chicago, Herbert was a bookworm. He liked baseball but had little interest in football. The local high school had fewer than twenty boys. He would have been pressed into football service anyhow, but he was too small, weighing under one hundred pounds. By the time the family moved to the equally small town of Medotta, he had grown enough to play a lackluster role as an end.

In the fall of 1917 Crisler arrived at the University of Chicago on an academic pre-med scholarship. He had no intention of pursuing any sports. As he later told it, one day he was standing on the sidelines watching a football practice. The coach, Amos Alonzo Stagg, was backpedaling while watching the scrimmage and accidentally backed into him. As they picked themselves up, Stagg noticed the thin six-footer's freshman cap and said, "Why aren't you out for freshman football?"

"I've never played football," Crisler said.

"You ought to be out anyway with the rest of your classmates," said the already legendary coach.

Crisler accepted the challenge and the next day reported to the freshman coach, Pat Page. He was given a uniform and sent into the scrimmage.

"I took a terrible pounding," Crisler recalled. "That evening I turned in my uniform and quit the team."

About ten days later Crisler was walking on the campus when Stagg, riding a bicycle, came toward him. The student tried to duck out of sight, but Stagg spotted him.

"Weren't you out for football?" Stagg asked.

"Yes, but I quit. I don't know anything about the game."

Stagg gave him a scornful look. "I never thought you'd be a quitter," he said.

Crisler rose to the bait. "I'll show you," he muttered to himself. The next day he asked for his uniform back.

Years later Crisler reflected on how different his life would have been "if the old man hadn't come riding by on his bike at that precise moment that day."

By the time he graduated in 1922, Crisler had become one of only two Chicago students ever to earn nine varsity letters—as an end for Stagg, an all–Big Ten basketball guard, and a pitcher good enough to draw an offer from White Sox scout Ed Walsh. He also earned a nickname.

One day in practice Stagg watched Crisler's fumbles and mistakes mess up one play after another. "Crisler," Stagg barked, "you remind me of Fritz Kreisler, the great violinist, not because you resemble him but because you're so different. From now on, you're Fritz."

Under Stagg's guidance, Fritz Crisler began to look at football like a physician, as a diagnostic challenge: If we did this, what would the other side do? How do we defend against surprises they might try? How do you train young men to be spiritually as well as physically ready to do their best? He changed his major to psychology.

Stagg was a teacher of life as well as football. He emphasized clean, honest, by-the-rules football. The one-time divinity student at Yale was beloved on the campus, win or lose. He had been there for twenty-five years when Crisler arrived. The Chicago Maroons lost all six of their games in 1918, but there was no "Fire Stagg!" furor. Crisler was out of school that year, at an army officer-training facility, where he matured into the commanding presence that would characterize him for the rest of his life. He became captain of the basketball and baseball teams.

Football was evolving from the days when every play was

a power play into the line. The forward pass, quick kicks, laterals, spinners, and reverses were opening up the offenses and challenging defenses. Quickness and deception were replacing the massing of brawn (as much brawn as 165-pounders could amass) that plowed ahead like a snowplow in front of the man with the ball.

Twenty-five years later Crisler's playbook would contain over 170 plays. His complex system would require more brains than strength to execute.

The elite football teams were all in the East. Western games earned slight coverage and even slighter respect in the large eastern press. The serious football world began at Cambridge, went to New Haven, north through Dartmouth, Cornell, and Colgate, and ended in Pennsylvania. Rarely did a western team face one of the eastern elite.

In 1921 Stagg managed to schedule a game at Princeton. On October 22 he brought his small squad of underdog Maroons into Palmer Field and shocked the Tigers with a 9–0 victory. Crisler played all sixty minutes, convincingly containing Princeton's all-American tackle Stan Keck, who outweighed him by forty pounds. The *New York Times* found it noteworthy to point out the prominent part played by the forward pass in games of the day, including the one that scored Chicago's only touchdown.

Other western teams made appearances in the east that year, helping to advance the game's national stature.

After he graduated, Crisler stayed on as an assistant under Stagg, whose influence on him grew. The soft-spoken Stagg never swore, smoked, or drank. One day Crisler overheard Stagg telling an assistant, "Abusive language directed at a player is a rather futile way to urge him to do his best." Crisler smoked when Stagg wasn't looking and enjoyed his Scotch all his life, but he never swore or raised his voice. Well, hardly ever.

One of his Princeton players recalled, "When Fritz said 'damnation,' he was really mad and you better start ducking. Otherwise there was no swearing. He would light into you if you did wrong, but more like your father."

When Princeton came to Chicago for a return match on October 28, 1922, the rare appearance of an eastern team in the Midwest created a demand for tickets that exceeded one hundred thousand, three times the capacity of Stagg Field. Interest was so high that AT&T arranged the first long-distance radio broadcast of a football game back to the East.

Using powerful plunges through the Princeton line, Chicago built an 18–7 lead after three quarters. A Chicago fumble on a punt return was picked up and run for a Tiger touchdown. Late in the game Princeton scored again to take the lead, 21–18. With time running out, Chicago completed three passes to the Tiger six. Three thrusts through the line brought the Maroons within a few feet of the goal line.

Sitting beside Stagg, Crisler learned a lesson in fair play. He suggested the coach send in his son, Alonzo Jr., with instructions to try an end run. The coach said no, citing the rule book's "discouraging" of the use of substitutes to carry information to their teams. Fullback John Thomas dove into the line again and was stopped again, ending what Crisler later called the greatest exhibition of football he had ever seen.

The following year, when Knute Rockne brought his undefeated Notre Dame team to New York City for the first time to play Army and created millions of "subway alumni" fans of the Fighting Irish, college football attained the national stature it has built on ever since. "Real football" was no longer the exclusive province of the eastern schools that would come to be known as the Ivy League.

In 1925 Fritz Crisler was offered the head coaching position at Minnesota. Stagg told him, "You're not ready to fly." Crisler stayed and coached the baseball team as well for three years. When Minnesota called again in 1930, Stagg said, "You're ready now."

The first thing Crisler did was tour the area, meeting alumni, talking up the Gophers' football program, and recruiting players. It took him a year to revitalize football at Minnesota. In his first year the Gophers won only one conference game in a 3-4-1 season. In 1931 they were 7-3.

Princeton's football fortunes had declined since the power-houses of the early 1920s. Since the Tigers' 8-0 1922 season, they had not had a losing year until 1929. In 1930 and 1931 they had won their warm-up opener against Amherst and didn't beat anybody else. Following longtime coach Bill Roper's retirement after the disastrous 1930 season, a fierce debate broke out.

None of the Elite Three—Harvard, Yale, and Princeton—had ever gone outside their alumni for a football coach, not even for an assistant. The Princeton Football Association that ran the athletic program was divided. The old-timers said they had done all right with alumni coaches for sixty-two years; a few bad years was no reason to abandon tradition. The younger generation had less regard for tradition. An editorial in the student newspaper said, "*The Princetonian* has repeatedly disparaged the belief that adherence to the high standards of Princeton sportsmanship in a coaching position here is in any way contingent upon previous undergraduate connection with the university."

Bill Roper said the school was out of touch with the times. It needed an athletic director like Fielding Yost at Michigan.

The Football Association bent, but only if it could sign the most famous and successful coach in the country—Knute Rockne of Notre Dame. In January 1931 Rockne accepted Princeton's offer, but he soon changed his mind. Two months later he died in an airplane crash. The association then turned inward and persuaded basketball coach Al Wittmer to take the job. He quit after losing seven in a row, culminating in a 51–14 debacle in the Yale Bowl.

There were howls to give up football altogether. Princeton hadn't won a single major game in four years. The opposition to bringing in a non-grad gave up, either from hopelessness or indifference. The university took control of the athletic program and appointed a supervisor and graduate manager but kept the Football Association and selected a committee to search for a new coach.

One of the advantages that Fritz Crisler had going for him was the reputation of Alonzo Stagg. As a disciple of Stagg's, he was considered most likely to "fit in" with the general scheme of things at Old Nassau. Now a suave, polished, urbane gentleman of thirty-three, he looked as if he could pass for a distinguished physician—or even a Princeton man.

One insider said that Crisler impressed the search committee "because he was intelligent, of an appealing personality, and seemed to have the same ideas on the general scheme of things that have been those of Princeton. At Chicago he learned to make the best of limited material, short practice sessions, and to face many of the problems a football coach will have at Princeton. He seems well fitted, by personality and experience, to handle the Princeton job."

On the search committee's recommendation, Princeton president John G. Hibben telephoned Crisler at Minnesota and offered him the job. The boy from Earlville said calmly, "I'll be glad to accept if you'll put it in writing."

"To be perfectly honest," he recalled, "I was flattered as hell that Princeton came after me, a corn-fed yokel. What really clinched the decision for me, though, was the obvious fact that all business, publicity, and prestige faced east in the early 1930s."

Crisler needed all his command and presence when he arrived in Princeton on March 1, 1932, to discuss his three-year contract. Before sunrise the next morning he was driving around the town in a borrowed car looking for the train station when a policeman pulled him over and took him to the police station. Unknown to Crisler, the Lindbergh baby had been kidnapped the night before ten miles away in Hopewell. The police had been alerted to stop anyone acting suspiciously. They listened to Crisler's story but wouldn't release him until the car's owner came down and vouched for him.

In addition to his football duties, Crisler would coach the basketball team for the first two years. He brought three assistants with him: Tad Wieman, line coach who had been a head coach at Michigan; end coach Campbell Dickson, who had played for Stagg; and backfield coach Earl Martineau from Minnesota.

The old guard might have grudgingly accepted a non-grad with the stature of a Knute Rockne or Alonzo Stagg, even though Stagg was an—ugh!—Yale man. But who was Fritz Crisler? Two undistinguished years at Minnesota were all he had behind him. Aware of the opposition, Crisler set out to sell himself by visiting as many alumni clubs as he could. And recruited as he went.

The peskiest alum that Crisler would have to deal with was F. Scott Fitzgerald, class of 1917. The five-foot-seven, 138-pound Fitzgerald had been on the freshman team for three days when he turned an ankle and never showed up again. Now he would call the coach from the West Coast at all hours, offering advice and suggestions, which Crisler would—usually politely—ignore.

Fifty-six men turned out for the start of spring practice on April 4. End Ben Delaney recalled that Crisler "made it loud and clear: 'I'm from the Midwest. I'm not a Princetonian. You guys have that position, but we're going to work together.' He did a fantastic job of giving you what you needed and had an amazing group of coaches. No easterners, but all excellent students of the game." It would take about three years before Crisler assumed the position of being a Princetonian.

At the end of spring practice Crisler gave them a five-week course of conditioning exercises. Under a Big Three agreement, fall practice could not begin before September 15. In a September 1932 Alumni Weekly, Crisler contributed an essay on the place of athletics in education. Perhaps remembering his introduction to the sport at Chicago, he wrote, "If any man wants coaching in football, he is entitled to it and can have it." Nobody would be cut.

Seventy men turned out.

Bill Roper railed against the new supervisor of sports for providing only one "light" opener against Amherst before sending the new coach up against a killer schedule of Columbia, Cornell, Navy, and Michigan. After defeating Amherst, 22–0, the Tigers lost predictably to Columbia, 20–7, then held a powerful Cornell team to a 0–0 tie and did the same to Navy a week later. They went to Michigan and barely lost, 14–7, to the Big Ten champions. After a 53–0 romp against Lehigh, they battled Yale to a 7–7 tie, ending the most successful 2-2-3 season in history. Crisler was hailed as a miracle man. He had revived the old Tiger spirit, building morale along with timing, speed, and coordination.

Crisler's style in the dressing room was intense but low key, even solemn. Like Rockne, his pre-game and halftime talks tended to be emotional. Underlying them was an understanding of each man and the need for mental and physical discipline. He would turn on the waterworks—"He could tear you to shreds," said one player—if he thought there was a need for it. Otherwise, if they were playing their game, he had little to say at halftime. He applied his training in psychology and could be an adrenaline pumper. But there are no gauges on human glands to indicate when to quit pumping. Sometimes he overdid it and it backfired and made the team tighter. From the beginning of his time at Princeton, the Yale game seemed to bring this excess out in him.

Fred Russell of the *Nashville Banner* wrote a story of one such pep talk before a Yale game. As Crisler solemnly urged his team to "go out on that field hallowed by the blood of your grandfathers and fight," players sobbed. The coach choked up. As the players filed out, one of them paused, patted Crisler on the shoulder, and said, "Come on, toots, get hold of yourself."

Exaggerated? Probably. Point-making? Certainly.

After the '32 Yale 7–7 tie, Crisler said he was proud of the team for coming back to score a late touchdown after Yale had thwarted many goal-line assaults. "Tension was our greatest fault," he said. "The team was too tense when it entered the game and the tension never slackened. We were too eager when our scoring opportunities came."

Before the '33 game Crisler told his team, "I don't want any of you to speak to a single person when you leave this locker room to go on the field." End Gil Lea's sister was standing outside the locker room and waved and called, "Hi." Lea ducked his head and kept going.

In his first year Crisler had recruited the most talented freshman team in the school's history. The class of '36 squad was loaded with prep school captains, who waltzed through the season undefeated, untied, and unscored upon. They defeated the Yale freshmen, 3–0, for the first time in years.

Amid warnings from academia that football was assuming too much importance on college campuses, Yale announced it was considering cutting out spring practice and reducing the football schedule while putting more emphasis on intramural sports. Crisler commented, "In regard to reducing the so-called over-emphasis on football, I think we've got too much over-emphasis on the over-emphasis of football."

When he read a claim that athletes would study more if they were relieved of the burden of daily practice, Crisler decided to test that theory. He gave all the players a day off, then surveyed them to see what they had done with their time. Twenty-four watched freshman practice, eleven engaged in miscellaneous diversions, nine went to the movies, eight partook of recreational pursuits, and three studied.

Success in any field breeds imitators. Notre Dame's success in the 1920s had led many coaches to adopt what was called the "Notre Dame box," which enhanced Rockne's innovative use of the forward pass. The box had a balanced line with two backs behind the center—either one could take the snap—and two just behind the line. They frequently shifted before the ball was snapped, confusing the defense.

By the 1930s some coaches were turning away from the box. Fritz Crisler brought the single wing to Princeton. Similar to today's shotgun, it had many variations. Crisler favored an unbalanced line with three backs lined up in front and to the right of the quarterback. For every game he introduced new plays and deceptive tricks. Once in his first game against Yale the entire line lined up to the right of the center, making him an end. The defense looked for him to become a pass receiver. He was a decoy; it became a statue of liberty play that didn't work. The ball carrier was thrown for an 11-yard loss. Crisler also tried a sleeper play, known then as a "shoestring" because the player went near the sidelines and tried to unobtrusively bend down as though tying his shoestrings.

Augmented by the sensational freshmen of '32, the 1933 Tigers were a deep, formidable army. Crisler had three full teams, and he preferred to substitute an entire fresh team instead of one or two men at a time. This year they had two light openers, easily blowing out Amherst and Williams before facing their first real test, Columbia. At the start of the week Crisler put up a large cardboard panel in Osborn Field House with photos of the Columbia players aligned in their positions. Each Princeton starter picked out his counterpart and studied his picture each day.

Columbia coach Lou Little's plan was to take an early lead and dig in against the waves he knew Crisler would throw at him. It didn't work. The Columbia halfback took the opening kickoff and was hit so hard he lost the football and Princeton recovered. Five plays later the Tigers scored. Sophomore halfback Garry LeVan followed his powerful interference for two touchdowns and the defense held Columbia scoreless, 20–0.

Princeton roared through nine opponents, ending with a 27–2 rout of Yale in New Haven. Nobody scored on the Tigers until their eighth game. They rolled up 217 points and surrendered 8. And they received an invitation to play Stanford in the Rose Bowl in Pasadena. The team wanted to go. More than one-third of the student body signed a petition in favor of going. But the administration, citing a pact among the Big Three to play no post-season games, said no.

Columbia, beaten only by Princeton, went instead and upset Stanford, 7–0.

Fritz Crisler looked ahead to the 1934 season with every reason to anticipate another unblemished record.

4 | Greasy Neale

THE ONLY THING ALFRED EARLE NEALE WANTED IN LIFE WAS to be a professional baseball player. Sure, he played football and basketball too, but only to keep busy until it was warm enough to swing a bat again.

Born November 5, 1891, in Parkersburg, West Virginia, he dropped the "Alfred" as soon as he could and was known as Earle when he quit school in the ninth grade and went to work as a grease boy in a steel mill. One day in a kids' taunting match, he called a boy who never washed "Dirty Face." The other kid called him "Greasy." The name stuck; it was a measure of the man that despite the wealth and renown he achieved, he never tried to lose it. Twenty years later, when the Pooh-Bahs of Yale starchily requested that the gentlemen of the press refer to their new coach as Earle, he said nothing doing. They should continue to call him Greasy if they wanted to.

After two years of working sixteen hours a day for $12.50 a week, Greasy had enough of the steel mill and went back to school. The high school didn't have a football coach. At nineteen, Greasy was the oldest, so he took charge of the team. He found he enjoyed teaching, rousing the younger boys' fighting spirits and goading them on to garrison finishes.

Neale broke into minor league baseball as an outfielder in 1912 and accepted a football scholarship to West Virginia Wesleyan in the fall. He was a freshman end on a team that went 7-0. He played basketball and once scored 39 points at a time when most teams didn't score half that many in a game. That summer he batted .335 in the Class C Canadian League.

Neale left Wesleyan in 1914, played ball the next two summers, and coached the Muskingum College football team each fall. In 1915 he batted .351 at Wheeling in the Central League and was purchased by the Cincinnati Reds. He led all players with 10 hits in the 1919 World Series—which he later called the highlight of his athletic career—and played his last major league game in 1924.

In the meantime he returned to coaching at West Virginia Wesleyan College in the fall of 1916. He had a flair for inventing spectacular trick plays. Some historians credit him with being the first to use man-to-man pass coverage. He didn't hesitate to copy a new bit of trickery when he saw it. Years later he said, "I think I was a success as a coach because I wasn't afraid to borrow what had worked for somebody else. People in the stands never ask you where you got it. They only want to know if you got it." (Many coaches, including Crisler and Neale, went to pro games on Sundays and took notes on plays they might be able to use.)

In 1917 he scored the first great upset of his career. Wesleyan was considered a "cream puff" on the West Virginia annual schedule. On November 14 on a snow-covered field, Neale sent his three-touchdown underdogs against the Mountaineers. Using the single-wing formation, which facilitated double and triple and fake reverses (called the "criss cross" at that time), Neale used those plays with deadly effect all afternoon, crushing the Mountaineers, 20–0.

He was also playing professional football on Sundays. Pro football was a disorganized enterprise in those pre-NFL days. Neale joined the Canton Bulldogs under the name Foster because the Reds frowned on their ballplayers engaging in other sports. But he didn't fool anybody. The Reds chose to look the other way. The Bulldogs never practiced during the week. The coach was 1912 Olympics hero Jim Thorpe, but Greasy Neale ran the team on the field. Before each game Thorpe would ask each player how much he could play. Some said, "Thirty minutes," others more or less. Neale always said, "Put me down for sixty."

That was the extent of Thorpe's coaching. On the field the Bulldogs used a huddle, not a widespread practice at the time. But since they never practiced, that was the only way they could figure out what to do. Even though Thorpe played, the quarterback, former Dartmouth All-American Milt Ghee, usually asked Greasy what play to run.

After the 1919 World Series, Neale coached football and baseball at Marietta College while playing for the Reds for two years.

During that time his football teams went nine games without giving up a score. In 1920 they upset Michigan State, 23–7, and Cincinnati, 20–0, losing only to Boston College.

A little over two years after playing in the World Series, Greasy Neale was coaching a team in the Rose Bowl. In 1921 he went to Washington & Jefferson, a small college in Pennsylvania where the football team comprised 10 percent of the entire student body. The small pool of talent didn't faze him. "Granted certain physical endowments, a boy can be successful through application and determination," he said. He was cocky and he wanted his players to be that way. He let them know, "If a player doesn't think he's the best man on the field, I don't want him on the team."

Neale's boys went to war for him with a fierce defense that rarely gave up more than one or two first downs as they marched over much bigger opponents: West Virginia, Pitt, Syracuse, Bucknell. In their last game against Detroit they gave up a total of 4 yards rushing.

Other, bigger schools—Cornell, Lafayette, Penn State—were also undefeated that year, but to everyone's surprise and some people's indignation, the 1922 Rose Bowl invitation went to the W&J Presidents.

Only Greasy Neale and the nineteen players who made the trip thought they deserved to be there or had a chance against the mighty California Golden Bears. San Francisco sportswriter Jack James summed up the attitude on the West Coast: "The only thing I know about Washington and Jefferson is that they are both dead."

"Nobody thought we had a chance," Neale recalled. "But I knew what we could do. I told everybody Cal wouldn't score on us. They just laughed."

In a battle of punts on a muddy field, Cal managed only two first downs. The only touchdown, a 35-yard run off a fake punt by W&J's Wayne Brenkert, was called back by an offside penalty. Two W&J field goal attempts failed, and the game ended 0–0.

The Presidents' eleven starters played the entire sixty minutes.

The following fall W&J lost only one game, to Pitt. It broke a Lafayette sixteen-game undefeated streak, fighting back from a 13–0 halftime deficit. That's when Neale introduced the fake reverse, telling the quarterback to turn his back to the defense and fake a handoff to a back crossing in front of him. The quarterback found himself all alone and ran for a touchdown. They then used the old (even then) statue of liberty play to tie the game and made the extra point on a pass (either a kick or a play was worth one point).

With some trepidation and his big league playing days nearing the end, Greasy Neale signed to coach the University of Virginia in 1923. He didn't know how his rough-hewn, no-frills personality would go over with the Cavaliers. And he wasn't about to change, couldn't change even if they tried to make a gentleman out of him. What he found was more indifference than hostility. There was a general lack of enthusiasm for football. The students didn't care. Attendance was poor. He stayed six years and had a winning record, but nothing changed, including Greasy. After a 2-6-1 1928 season he resigned.

Greasy returned to his first love, baseball, in 1929 as a coach with the St. Louis Cardinals, and in 1930 he went back to the bush leagues as a playing manager at Clarksburg in the Class C Middle Atlantic League, batting .332 at the age of thirty-eight. That fall, after twelve years on the sidelines, he coached the Ironton, Ohio, semi-pro football team and put himself in the lineup against the NFL's Portsmouth team. Outweighed by more than forty pounds, he came out of it suffering only a black eye in a 16–15 victory. Ironton also defeated the New York Giants and Chicago Bears in exhibition games.

When the West Virginia Mountaineers offered Neale the head coaching job in 1931, you'd have thought he'd be a natural: native son, rough as a mountain trail, talking their language. But his appointment drew explosive opposition. For one thing, he was following the school's greatest all-around athlete, Ira "Bull" Rodgers, as coach. For another, the attitude of Rodgers and the administration had been one of holding themselves aloof from the players and fans, like tin gods. That was clearly not Greasy Neale's style. He was about more than football, teaching fair play and an understanding and appreciation of life itself. He liked to mix with his players, socialize in their frat houses, and get to know them. He wanted them to understand that if he yelled at them—and he would, loudly, crudely, and often—it only meant he was interested in them. What they thought about the language he used was unimportant to him.

If he couldn't be a pal to his players and still maintain their respect as their coach, he said, they could have the job.

Some of his pre-game pep talks became legendary. His 148-pound center, Ben Schwartzwalder, later a longtime coach at Syracuse, said, "Greasy Neale tried to tell us three weeks running to go out and win the game for his dying mother, and there she was every game, sitting up in the stands."

Neale lasted three years. After a 3-5-3 record in 1933 he was fired.

The Yale alumni were restless, and when the football fanatics inhabiting the Yale Clubs around the nation became restless, they resembled awakening volcanoes. In the glory days of the 1920s, when they had once gone eighteen games without a loss, the New York City club celebrated wins over Harvard by tying up traffic in New York while hundreds of delirious sons of Eli poured out of their club headquarters on Forty-Fourth Street and paraded across Fifth Avenue to the Harvard Club on Forty-Third.

Now, after two mediocre years, ending with one-sided losses to Princeton and Harvard under their former freshman coach, Reggie Root, they demanded change. They clamored not just for a new coach, but for the overthrow of the hallowed tradition of appointing only alumni to run the football program. Princeton had done it, bringing in Fritz Crisler. Now the Tigers were the national champions. Dartmouth had just done it, hiring West Point graduate Red Blaik, Army's backfield coach for seven years. Other schools were recruiting big names: Elmer Layden at Notre Dame, Michigan All-American quarterback and pro-football star Benny Friedman at City College of New York.

The eight-man advisory football committee included Malcolm Farmer, manager of the Athletic Board of Control. The committee voted 6–2 to bring in an outsider. After all, it argued, the president of Yale didn't have to be an alumnus. (James Allen, the current president, was a Michigan and Harvard graduate.) Why should the football coach? The committee members had plenty of suggestions: Bernie Bierman, who had succeeded Crisler at Minnesota; Harry Kipke of Michigan; Lou Little at Columbia. Five of them favored hiring Kipke and all his assistants; one voted for Ossie Solem of Iowa. Or if it had to be a Yale graduate, bring back Tad Jones, Yale's most successful coach, who had retired in 1927. Or just hire all of the Michigan assistants, without Kipke, bringing Michigan's offensive and defensive schemes with them.

But Farmer and the Board of Control held the power, and they were adamant: no outsider would be the head coach at Yale. The head coach must be one of them, and Ducky Pond was their choice.

Farmer was ready for a rumpus when he announced on February 1, 1934, the advancement of Raymond "Ducky" Pond to lead the Bulldogs, and he got it. Pond, who had been known as Ducky since his student days at Hotchkiss, was remembered as

the hero of the 1923 win over Harvard. In a game played in pour-
ing rain, he had picked up one of the many fumbles and run 67
yards for Yale's first touchdown against Harvard in seven years.
The next year he led Yale in another rain-soaked defeat of Harvard. A short, stocky but speedy athlete, Pond had also been the
ace pitcher on the baseball team.

After two years' coaching at Hotchkiss, Pond had coached
Yale's scrub teams and scouted for the varsity since 1928. He
was popular but had no varsity coaching experience. Observers lavished him with lukewarm support. The best that could
be said for him was that he was a nice, quiet, uninspiring guy
on and off the field. There would be no pep talks, nothing with
more fighting spirit than a recitation of the alma mater, out of
Ducky Pond.

The alumni were not surprised, nor were they pleased by the
announcement. And they weren't surprised when Farmer also
announced the much-rumored appointment of Earle "Greasy"
Neale as backfield coach. Farmer knew that Greasy Neale was
available to provide what Pond lacked. He knew all about Neale's
experience and achievements. (Well, nearly all. There's no telling how the Yale potentates would have reacted if they'd been
aware that back in 1922 Neale had been fined $100 by baseball
commissioner Kenesaw Mountain Landis for signing a secret salary agreement with the Phillies.) Greasy's brother William had
played football for Yale in 1922–23 and was now the secretary for
intramural sports. But the alumni *were* surprised when Farmer
said that the coaching staff would include two other non-grads:
line coach Denny Myers, who had played at Iowa and been with
Neale for two years, and one-time Michigan captain Ivan Williamson, now a high school coach, as end coach. Farmer had orig-
inally hired Williamson as the freshman coach and Michigan
assistant Bennie Oosterbann as end coach. But when Michigan
athletic director Fielding Yost learned that Oosterbann would

be joining a mix of a Yale head coach and West Virginia back-field coach, he advised him not to take the job. Williamson was raised to end coach.

They were all hired for one year. The importance of Neale is reflected in his $6,000 salary, only $500 less than Pond's. Myers received $3,000, Williamson $2,500.

Some observers considered the lineup an improvement and hoped, for Pond's sake as well as Yale's, that it would succeed. Ralph Bloomer, a 1900 tackle, called Neale "a first-class strategist." The harshest criticism came from men who had won their football letters at Yale. Cupe Black, 1916 captain, snorted, "It's an awful joke." Another former captain said, "I don't think they have provided Yale with the teaching staff in football that is comparable to that of the teams the Yale players must face next fall. I would hate to be a Yale football man next season."

A letterman who wished to remain anonymous was blunter. "I think it is a crime to put Ducky Pond on the spot like that. Ducky is a nice kid. Everyone likes him. But, with assistants drawn from three different systems of play and one of those assistants a much older man and a former head coach himself, I can't see where Ducky or Yale football can go anywhere but out of the picture. There's no more hope for Ducky than there was for Reggie Root last year."

"Pond is the third head coach selected without previous varsity experience," said a New York Yale Club spokesman. "He may measure up to the job with the help he is getting from a seasoned coach like Earle Neale, but it is simply another noble experiment for the sake of an outworn policy."

John Reed Kilpatrick, president of Madison Square Garden who had played at Yale twenty-five years earlier, said, "[Pond's] a fine boy but I think it is too heavy a responsibility to throw on someone just out of college and who has had all his coaching experience under the Yale system of which I disapprove."

The *Yale Daily News* called it a practical arrangement that preserved "Yale sportsmanship," whatever that was.

"I'm tickled to death to be here," said Greasy Neale.

The alumni would remain untickled to death with the arrangement until it became evident that this would be Greasy Neale's team, not Ducky Pond's.

It's not clear whose idea it was to seek out Major Frank A. Wandle as Yale's new trainer, but soon after spring practice began it was evident that a new trainer was needed. Wandle had a soft spot in his heart for Yale, and when the call came, he eagerly took the job, even though it meant leaving coach Biff Jones, with whom he had served at West Point before joining Jones at LSU in 1932.

Respected throughout the athletic world for more than thirty years, Wandle was a man of calm, confidence, and cheerful countenance. During the Great War he had served as a recreation officer, and in 1918 he had supervised hundreds of army athletes at a Knights of Columbus Olympiad at Camp Dix, New Jersey. He was an exception in the days of ironing out knotted muscles with a rolling pin. He had extensive medical knowledge. In addition to setting broken fingers and mending bruised and bloody faces, Wandle preached injury prevention and supervised weight maintenance during the playing season. He was as much philosopher as bonesetter, tending to the spiritual and psychological needs of his athletes. He wrote the rules of conduct as well as the training regimen.

In recent years he had introduced a water wagon on rubber tires that he would roll out during a time-out or player injury. It was really more of a first aid cart; Major Wandle did not approve of his players drinking water during a game.

Wandle was considered in football circles the finest trainer in the business. His $7,125 salary was the highest in the athletic

department. (Talk about tradition: in the 1890s, Yale's star players stood in the gym to be rubbed down; forty years later Major
Wandle's salary would be listed under the heading "Rubbing"
in Yale's expense ledgers.)

Wandle would prove to be worth every cent of it.

5 | Spring 1934

WHEN FRITZ CRISLER OPENED HIS 1934 SPRING PRACTICE
at Princeton, he beheld what syndicated columnist Damon Runyon said was enough football players "to supply half a dozen
colleges." Nineteen lettermen were back, including the entire
first and second backfields from the '33 national champions. Another undefeated freshman team had joined them. There were
more than twenty high school and prep school captains among
them—so many that some of them had a tough time making
the number 3 team.

But Crisler had joined the growing ranks of football coaches
who accented the negative in their public comments. He was re-
ferred to as "Fritz the Reticent" and "Mr. Gloom." He had nothing ill to say about his offense, but "our defense is not as strong
as last year." He had lost his standout tackles, Charlie Ceppi
and Art Lane, to graduation and was concerned about replacing
them. As for the undefeated freshmen, "You never know how
good sophomores might be."

The picture in New Haven was markedly different. Spring
practice at Yale had never been taken seriously by either the
coaches or players. In spring other things caught a Yale man's
fancy. Football wasn't a business, a means to an end for the players. It was fun to play in the fall, not to work at year round. It
wasn't anybody's primary purpose for being there. Nobody had
an athletic scholarship. Some had academic scholarships and

were required to hold a job, like waiting on tables, and to sign a pledge that they weren't getting any aid or assistance from anyone other than the scholarship board. Staying in school depended on grades, not blocking and tackling. Perhaps that's why they had gained a reputation for being less than fierce on the football field. Newspapers called them "smilers" who displayed a jovial good nature during their games. At the same time, the players wanted to do well, and for the past several years there had been complaints about the coaching. They knew they were not being adequately prepared for the caliber of teams they faced, and they didn't keep it to themselves.

Successful coaches knew that the fundamentals had to be taught in spring practice; there was barely enough time in the fall to learn the plays and defenses before the first game. If the fundamentals weren't there already, it was a blueprint for a long, losing season.

Ducky Pond knew all that. He knew how things had been at Yale for the past few years. Greasy Neale and his fellow immigrants from the Midwest were not prepared for it. For whatever reason—to explain the Ivy attitude to the newcomers, to rally the troops or warn them—Pond wrote the following call to colors. It appeared in mid-February in the *Alumni Weekly*, but it was clearly aimed at the football team on campus.

> The attitude of the Yale boy is slightly different from that of the boy at most colleges. The Yale boy plays football because he likes to and not because his sojourn in college depends upon it. And he plays to win regardless of how his remarks may be misinterpreted at times by others. [This was a reference to a comment made by a Yale captain of a few years earlier, after a losing season, to the effect that winning wasn't everything.]
>
> The attitude toward football as being a seasonal sport has been responsible for the fact that we have never had a very successful spring practice.

Spring practice is regarded by most of our other colleges as being of great importance. It is the football period during which most of the hard work is done, such as fundamentals, blocking, tackling, scrimmaging and all the rough contact work. Yale, to have a successful season next fall, must rally to spring football—must realize that to win Yale must be football conscious the year round.

I believe the staff of assistant coaches appointed to be exceptionally strong. In Neale we have a man thoroughly experienced, one who knows football from every angle, versed in fundamentals, strategy and techniques. He knows how to get the most out of his men and I feel the boys will like him.

Myers and Williamson, though young, are experienced, and both are capable of demonstrating exactly what they teach. They are in as good condition as when they played—full of enthusiasm and gifted with personalities which will enable them to get the most out of their men.

It seemed as if Pond was trying to sell the new staff to the players as much as to the alumni.

The coaches were introduced to the players on March 1 at the Ray Tompkins House in a meeting led by Malcolm Farmer. Farmer expressed his confidence in the new staff if the players would show their cooperation, a plea that probably startled Greasy Neale. *Asking* for his players' cooperation was definitely not his style. Farmer then advised the players that if they had any problems or complaints, they should keep quiet or take their complaints to Ducky Pond. Many of Yale's most promising seasons had been ruined, he said, by criticism, often uncalled for.

Ducky Pond announced that there would be only light workouts until after spring vacation. The coaches would remain on the field every afternoon as long as there were men to coach, which made it sound as if it was up to the players, not the coaches, to decide when practice was over.

Practice would begin with two weeks of body-building exercises in the gym, led by swimming coach Bob Kiphuth.

Greasy Neale had a more rigorous plan in mind. He was eager to launch four weeks of intensive blocking and tackling drills beginning March 16. He wouldn't predict what kind of team they would have until he had a chance to look over the material he had to work with.

It's always difficult to introduce a radical change in system and philosophy to a football team. Yale's new staff had to weave together the Yale way with threads from Iowa, Michigan, and West Virginia. And Army.

Major Wandle strode into the gym like a new drill sergeant and immediately took charge. He barked commands at the physical therapists, Jimmy and Eddie O'Donnell, who were popular with the players. Resentments built. They were used to doing the usual exercise routines—knee bends and jumping up and down in place. Wandle emphasized more aerobics and stretching. A big, bulky man in his fifties, he led the strenuous exercises, doing them right along with the young athletes. "We all thought he would kill himself doing it," Larry Kelley recalled.

The major shocked the bean counters by the amount of money he spent reorganizing and equipping the training facilities. Among other things, he ordered a whirlpool tub and motor at a cost of $60 (remember, these were 1934 dollars). When it arrived, nobody could figure out how to heat the water. They had to ask the inventor who sold it to them how to work it. Wandle ordered all new uniforms from A. G. Spalding.

Wandle's style didn't make him popular, but he didn't care. His mission was to make every player tough enough to play sixty minutes of every game, conditioned enough to avoid injuries, mentally prepared for any situation, healthy enough to miss no game or practice. He was proud of his 1929 Army team, whose starters had played the entire game without a substitution in a 7–0 loss to Notre Dame on a cold, windy November 30 in Yankee Stadium. His twenty-page "Training Rules and Hints" covered nutrition, energy, endurance, coordination, attitude—the works. He overlooked nothing, from hair washing (once a week) to toenail clipping (close and straight across), how to drink milk, how much to eat, posture, training rules, and exercises.

It didn't take long for the culture of the Midwest to clash with the laid-back Ivies. At the first session, near the end of spring break, Neale noticed that several of the returning varsity and many of the freshmen were absent. Neale asked where they were. One was in Bermuda with his folks. Somebody else was in Florida. Another one had gone home.

"For God's sake, what goes on here?" Neale asked. "We've got football practice. What are these guys doing in Florida and Bermuda? They should be here."

Ducky Pond laughed it off. "They'll be here when we need them."

"Ducky Pond understood the Yale temperament," said '34 captain Clare Curtin, "and was a good buffer between us and the new coaches."

After freshman football season, Larry Kelley had played basketball and was now playing first base on the baseball team. In four years he would never show up for spring practice. (He didn't show up in class much more often. One spring day the academic dean, Mr. Paradise, summoned him for a meeting. The dean pulled out a file from a drawer and said, "You may be interested to know there's only one person in Yale who has cut more classes than you have." Kelley laughed and said, "Gee, I thought I was number one." Mr. Paradise said, "He hasn't even come back from Christmas vacation yet." Kelley got the message.)

Other freshmen, learning that spring practice meant ten

days of drilling on fundamentals, blocking and tackling, ran to join the track team to get out of it.

Neale was impatient. He was expected to install an entirely new offense and teach the quarterback how to call the plays and the backfield how to execute them, and he had no idea of who could do what.

Neale put the players through the toughest spring drills they'd ever seen. Line coach Denny Myers was a rough, tough character who wanted them to play that way—hard hitting but clean. He had them knocking heads from the start. Ivan Williamson was a thorough teacher who soon gained the linemen's respect. None of them was used to coaches expressing themselves in the salty style of Greasy Neale. Fifty years later lineman Bob "Chooch" Train recalled that Greasy Neale's use of language made Mickey Mantle sound like an English professor. One day Neale didn't like the way one of his backs was blocking. "God damn it," Neale said, "you couldn't block a sick whore off a pisspot."

Coaches didn't talk that way at Choate or Peddie or Hotchkiss—or Yale.

It didn't shock all of them. Lineman Paul Benjamin "Ben" Grosscup was a tough mountaineer from West Virginia. He was used to the Greasy Neales of the world. So was Larry Kelley, who came from the Pennsylvania coal country.

Halfback Stan Fuller didn't like the rough scrimmaging and spoke up. He told Neale it was silly to take a chance on getting hurt in spring scrimmages.

"He put me on the second team," Fuller said, "and I thought, 'That's it.' That queered me with him. I never talked to him after that."

But Neale talked plenty to Fuller and didn't let it influence his assessment of Fuller's abilities.

Jerry Roscoe was the holdover quarterback. A sophomore in '33, he had started the season as a 156-pound blocking back and became the quarterback in the third game. Reggie Root used the Notre Dame box; the offense was almost entirely on the ground. Roscoe rarely threw a pass. He and Neale met every day that spring. Neale explained the single-wing system he would be using, the kinds of plays they would be running, what to use in certain situations: down, field location, score, time left, etc. "Have a reason for what you're doing in each situation," he said. "If you're using a play or a series of plays that are very similar and it's working, keep on using it. Why stop what they can't stop? Once, twice, if it's still gaining, use it again. Keep an eye out. The only thing that can stop it is for them to change what they're doing. When they change, there will be a weakness somewhere else. Then exploit the other weakness."

Neale's job amounted to training a college junior to be the kind of offensive coordinator that today takes years as a player and assistant coach—and doing it in seven months. (The quarterback would be directing the defense too.) That summer he would conduct a correspondence course in strategy, sending Roscoe, Tom Curtin, and Ed King general and specific guidelines for play-calling, situational questions, and comments on their answers.

Neale also had to assess the abilities of the backs, design plays that might work, and teach the backs how to execute them. But that would have to wait until the fall practice, when he'd have three weeks to do it before the first game of what was considered the most suicidal schedule the Bulldogs had ever faced.

6 | Quarterbacks Class

Jerry Roscoe went home to San Diego that summer with a small, ring-bound notebook in which about thirty plays were diagramed. Each play had a number. Play 42, for instance, would mean the 4 back in the 2 hole. An 8 would be a sweep around one end, a 9 around the other.

Deception was a big part of the football playbooks of the time: double reverses and laterals, fake and real, fake punts, the statue of liberty. Timing was the key to their success. Neale had a favorite he called the dance play. The quarterback took the snap (always in what is now called the shotgun formation), turned his back to the line, faked to the fullback and wingback and kept the ball, took a few shuffle steps to the left, then went naked around left end. Greasy liked it for use anywhere on the field and urged Roscoe to use it "not only once in a football game, but three or four times." Roscoe was skeptical. He said it would be a giveaway to the defense. The coach urged him to use it, but once they were out on the field, it was his game to call.

One page of Roscoe's notebook had a layout of a football field marked by zones. Opponent's goal line to the 20: "scoring zone—special scoring plays"; 20 to 40: "use best ground-gaining plays"; 40 to 40: "kick fourth down"; 40 to own 20: "maneuvering plays—forward passes, end runs"; own 40 to 20: "kick third down"; 20 to goal line: "danger zone—kick second down."

These notes accompanied the layout:

> What plays you would use from your own 25 yard line up to your 40 yard line—with score tied use safe plays and kick on third down; score against you last half open up your attack; with your team ahead use extremely safe plays, kick on third down; with less than 3 minutes to play, end of half or end of game try to hold the ball.

What plays you would use from your own 40 yard line to your opponent's 40 yard line—With score tied you may start to open up, but do not use any flat passes that there is a chance of interception; if you do not think on third down that you can make first down kick; with score against you open up, use plays that you believe in your mind will fool the opponents; with your team ahead play the safe game, kick on third down.

What plays you would use from opponent's 40 yard line to their 10 or 15—With score tied open up; use plays that have been working for you, also use the same plays with score against you; with your team ahead use the straight running attack and if necessary on third down forward pass; with second down, one yard or less to go use a long pass; from your opponent's 15 yard line use the dead trap play; if you gain five or six yards continue with your running attack; if you gain less than three yards use ten or eleven lateral passes or dance play on second down; third down 29 forward pass or 28 and 22. Fourth down, goal to go, either place kick or drop kick according to the score, or if you are not in position use one of the passes which I mentioned on third down. Never at any time inside your opponent's ten or 15 yard line after you have made up your mind to use a series of plays fail to use them.

You must always think of the time to play, the end of half or the end of game, with the score tied, opponents ahead, or in your favor, any position on the field. Watch their defence always and do not let them over-shift on you.

In low-scoring games, the kicking game became all-important. The idea was to keep the other team out of your territory and improve field position with each exchange of punts. A punt out of bounds inside the ten was a deadly weapon, something kick receivers—often the quarterback—tried to guard against by shading toward one sideline to cut it off while staying far enough toward the middle to cover a punt toward the other sideline. It wasn't easy. The prevalence of punting made a fake kick play more likely to succeed. One reason teams punted on second or third down was that the punter stood only eight to ten yards behind the line, not the fifteen yards of today. His blockers were light-weight wingbacks, trying to stop linebackers shooting through the middle. More kicks were blocked. The thinking was that if you kicked before fourth down and the kick was blocked and you recovered it, you had another chance to punt. The same principle applied to field goal attempts on third downs.

There was another reason for emphasis on the kicking game. When you were expected to play the entire game, endurance became a big factor. There were few time-outs, no two-minute warnings or commercial breaks, few incomplete passes or penalties to stop the clock. Everybody was in constant motion: run the play, quick huddle, run another. Offense took more out of a team than defense. Defense was a rest. Kicking on first down to get out of your own territory made the other team work harder. When both teams used that strategy, the exchanges of punts resembled a chess game, maneuvering to get into position to run effective offensive plays

From his sessions with Neale, Roscoe made the following notes:

If ever in doubt about anything, punt. Always save special plays to spring when there is a chance of scoring. If the score is even—in first period—defense closing in—never use pass. If defense is inviting it, of course pass. If we are winning, don't pass in the second quarter. Pass when near the other team's goal only as a last resort. Don't pass if running plays are working well. Keep head up about picking plays in sequence, such as 2, 7, 3 or 7, 8 etc. Unless he is the only man gaining at all on the play desired, never use the punter on the play before you wish him to punt. If a new man is sent in, never use him on the first play. Give him a chance to get used to the game. Shift backfield around often enough to keep the men from becoming too tired.

Neale believed in starting a game by kicking off whenever he had the choice to give his players a chance to settle down and get rid of the ubiquitous pre-game jitters while deep in the enemy's territory.

At least twice a month Neale sent out a quiz from his home in Lost Creek, West Virginia, to the three likely quarterbacks. The first one began, "Remember, as I have told you before that you must have your plan of attack in your own mind before you enter the game; you cannot after going on the field try to remember the things and the plays that I have instructed you to use at different points. Plan your attack this summer then when you are called upon to run the team you will be ready."

Question No. 1: "After receiving the kick-off at the beginning of the game and your team has returned the ball to your own 25-yard line, 1st down, 10 yards to go, what play would you use? 2nd down, 5 yards to go, what play would you use? 3rd down, 1 yard to go or less, would you kick or try for a first down?"

Jerry Roscoe's answer: "1st down, 10 yds to go, I would start off the game with the 7 play [a short yardage play between the right guard and tackle], and then, having gained 5 yds with it I'd come right back with the same play again on 2nd down. After making 9 yds in two plays I would be reasonably sure of a first down if I should try for it. My decision however would be made according to wind conditions. As a rule I would not kick under those conditions. 7 play again."

The coach marked that OK.

Question No. 2: "You have made a first down on your own 40-yard line. What play would you use in 1st down? On 2nd down you have 1 yard or less to go for a first down. What play would you use?"

Roscoe's answer: "I would continue to use the 7 play until it was stopped by my opponents, then I would open up with an 8 play [handoff to the wingback around right end] possibly if their tackle was crashing in, or try a 9 play [a fake handoff then a reverse by the wingback around left end]. 2nd down and one yard or less to go I'd use the 25 pass if their safety man were up close expecting a running play. This would also be good experimenting ground, setting up dance play, etc."

That drew an OK from the coach.

One response drew only a "Fair" from Neale. The question was, "What position on the field would you call one of the backfield men back with you on the 4th down when you were sure your opponents would kick?"

Roscoe wrote, "I would call a man back when my opponents were least apt to need protection for their own kicker and would release more men to come down immediately; in other words when I was back in my own territory."

Neale wrote beneath it, "To keep them from punting out of bounds."

In another set of questions, Neale urged his play-callers, "Do not study over these questions, answer them with confidence in yourself the same as you would decide on a play if the same situation presented itself on the football field."

Other quizzes emphasized Neale's approach to the kicking game, which was the thinking of even the most innovative offense-minded coaches of the time.

Example: "If the ball is in your possession on your opponent's 32-yard line, fourth down, five yards to go, what would be your plan of quarterback strategy at this point?"

Roscoe wrote, "25 pass over the goal line, making sure my passer were the best long passer at my disposal."

Neale responded: "Kick out of bounds with your team leading or tied. Your team behind use forward pass or play you think could make 5 yds with—such as 28 pass or dance play.—Your answer means that your passer must throw the ball 42 yds."

And so the education of the quarterbacks went on through the summer. They would be responsible for calling all the plays on offense and aligning the defense if a pass or punt was anticipated. If Roscoe thought the team needed a word of encouragement during the game, he would offer it. In the huddle, anyone who had an observation to make about the defense would speak up. For example, if they needed two or three yards and a lineman thought he could push his opponent back that far, he wouldn't hesitate to suggest running a play his way. Otherwise the quarterback was completely on his own. He would call the play by number and that was it.

7 | Fall 1934

FRITZ CRISLER DIDN'T HAVE A NEW SYSTEM TO INSTALL OR a new quarterback to train when fall football practice began September 15. But, in addition to plugging in two new tackles in the line, he did have a legitimate concern: motivation.

His veterans were intelligent, respected campus leaders, class and student body officers, members of exclusive eating clubs and secret societies. Fullback Pepper Constable had been his class's president for three years. He would graduate Phi Beta Kappa and win the school's highest undergraduate honor, the Pyne Prize. They were the big men on campus. They were all complete athletes. Most of them had been basketball, baseball, and track stars in prep school. They were good, even great football players.

And they knew it.

The scare that lightly regarded Washington and Lee (from

Lexington, Virginia) had given them in 1933 haunted Crisler. The experts had laughed when Crisler said he expected the W&L game to be a hard one. Same old Mr. Gloom, they said. In his Friday column of predictions, *New York Times* columnist John Kieran had written, "Why not have them all like this, just to simplify the picking? One dozen votes for the roaring Princeton Tiger." But they had barely escaped with their skins, eking out a 6–0 win. Twice W&L had recovered fumbles and run them in for touchdowns, only to have both called back by the referee's ruling that the ball was dead.Afterward Crisler had told them, "If you all would spend as much time and energy playing football as you do reading the newspapers about yourselves, you might turn into football players some day."

They had ended the season with another narrow escape, 7–0 over Dartmouth.

So Crisler began fall practice by knocking his own team and building up their opponents: "If we are not twenty percent better in all departments than last year we will lose at least three games," he told reporters. "All of our opponents are stronger than last year and are going to be tough. Washington and Lee is pointing at us. Cornell is planning to surprise its opponents. Harvard is greatly to be feared. Yale is really going to surprise people this year. They will have a great deal of reserve power [a comment that would have drawn a snort from Greasy Neale] and might beat Columbia."

Looking way ahead, Crisler feared a big letdown after the Yale game, win or lose, and worried about keeping team spirits up for the following week's finale against Dartmouth.

A virtuoso performance of his Mr. Gloom role, maybe, but its intent was clear: a preemptive strike against overconfidence.

Crisler greeted eighty candidates in Osborn Field House on September 14 and the next day began two-a-day drills until classes began on September 25, when they would cut back to one a day. As always with him, discipline came first. When star guard Jac Weller showed up a few days late, Crisler curtly stuck him on the second team. He stayed there for two weeks. When Weller questioned Crisler about it, the coach reminded him who was in charge. People who showed up late for practice had to be satisfied with whatever spot was still open. Then he reinstated Weller.

During the summer Crisler had sent out five letters to every man on the team, advising them on how to keep in the best condition for the coming season. A week before reporting, a dozen of them had gathered at Garry LeVan's home in Steubenville, Ohio, to work out. Still, when he looked them over on the first day, Crisler pronounced them all in "lousy shape." He was not going to let up on them. The way they looked to him, he said, they would start bad and go downhill from there.

Crisler believed that "tackling, blocking, and charging win football games." Those were the fundamentals they would work on every week of the season. The self-discipline he preached was not just for his teams. He wrote out his practice plans, plotting every step of every player in every play. Every practice session was planned to the minute.

On the first day Crisler, wearing a uniform with the number 34 on its back, led them through a two-hour session on Fitzpatrick Field. In the afternoon they switched to University Field, where backfield coach Earl Martineau had the backs charging low under a rope stretched between the goal posts.

Day after day they went through scrimmages, signal drills, and repetitive perfecting of their timing of the "Crisler shift." Crisler stood on a platform built across the goal post crossbar on University Field, looking down on the first team and the scrubs lined up beneath him. They would run the same play over and over, ten, fifteen, twenty times, while he commented and corrected each one on his footwork and blocking until they had it all together. Then they'd try it on another play. It went on for hours, finishing under the floodlights.

Veteran end Gil Lea explained the Crisler method:

We did everything precisely, even the way we looked. We were all dressed exactly alike, socks all exactly the same height. No other football team did it the way we did. Coming out of a huddle, we'd take one-two-three-four steps and land in a line, nine of us. The quarterback would say one, two hike, and on the hike we would each take two steps to our position, then one second later the play would start. The opponent didn't know what we were going to do from our first formation until we took those last two steps and then they had little time to react. On the first lineup we're about four or five feet back of the line. They had to scramble to get ready. They knew when the ball was going to be snapped; they knew the timing; but they didn't know where we were going to go in the final lineup. On a trap I was to take two steps exactly, as though I was going to take out the tackle, let him through and go for a back.

Coaches Weiman and Dickson taught the linemen how to fake instead of being faked. "In the case of a running back, fake him instead of him faking you out. Do the same with a kick receiver. Let the other guy guess which way you're going to come at him instead of going straight in."

Damon Runyon wrote, "Princeton's No. 3 team is almost as good as its team No. 2, and Team No. 2 is right up close to Team No. 1."

Fritz Crisler didn't thank him for the compliment. But there was no way he could play down the talent and depth of his forces.

Everyone in the backfield—from the five-foot-nine, 155-pound Garry LeVan to the 200-pound Pepper Constable—was a ferocious blocker and tackler. The fullback, Constable, plowed into the line like a runaway locomotive. A perfectionist, he demanded more of himself than any human could deliver. During a game he could be heard muttering to himself if he didn't execute a block or tackle up to his impossibly high standards. The elusive snake-hips halfback LeVan was the most dangerous open field runner in the land. He could punt, was perhaps the best passer as well as receiver on the team, and led in interceptions. Homer Spofford almost matched him for speed and agility. Quarterback John Paul "Katz" Kadlic needed no tutorial on calling plays. Kadlic and Constable were battering rams of interference for Spofford and LeVan. Halfback Ken Sandbach did the place kicking when he was in the game. He and Les Kaufman and Ippy Ruton-Miller were all good enough to be first string anywhere else in the country. Ruton-Miller's dad had been a fullback at Princeton thirty years earlier. Ippy kept things lively with his jokes and stories.

The middle of the line was anchored by the captain, center Elwood "Mose" Kalbaugh. (For unknown reasons, Princeton captains were traditionally middle linemen.) Kalbaugh was a quiet leader. He had started the 1933 season as the backup center. When the starter broke an ankle before the first game, Kalbaugh stepped in and became an impenetrable fortress all year. In the W&L game he had personally stuffed two attempts by the Generals to break through the line in a game-ending goal-line stand. His every snap of the ball was perfect, no small factor at a time when whoever was to take the snap stood several yards back on every play. He had earned the respect of the players and had been elected 1934 captain.

When Kalbaugh was bothered by a sore hip during the early weeks of practice, Crisler fretted that he had no backup center who could come close to filling his shoes.

Flanking Kalbaugh as guards were John "Jac" Weller and Frank John. Weller, a Jimmy Cagney look alike, at six-foot-one,

225 pounds, was one of the biggest linemen in Princeton history to that time. He had spent the summer digging ditches. He was also fast enough to outrun the ends down the field in pursuit of a kick receiver. A savage tackler, he stepped back as a linebacker on defense. Weller, from Jacksonville, Florida, kept the team loose with his tall tales—at least they sounded like tall tales—related in a slow drawl.

Frank John had worked as a waiter, bouncer in a campus club, and longshoreman.

It was easier to break through a brick wall with a teaspoon than penetrate Kalbaugh, Weller, and John.

Crisler could afford to move his primary punter, Hugh MacMillan, from the backfield to left end to alternate with the veteran Ben Delaney, who missed several weeks with chronic appendicitis. If there was any weakness, it was in the kicking game. MacMillan could be inconsistent. But it usually didn't matter when the Tiger was rolling up the yardage.

Gil Lea was the right end. Lea was the fourth generation of his family to play football at Princeton. He had been practicing tackling and blocking and falling on the ball since he was six years old. He had starred in hockey, baseball, track, tennis, and football at St. Paul's in New Hampshire.

LeVan, Constable, Weller, Kaufman, and Lea had all been part of the 1932 freshman team that had yet to taste defeat in an orange and black uniform.

Crisler's problem in replacing his pair of graduated tackles was not in finding someone but in choosing. He eventually settled on moving returning guard Dave Chamberlain and George Stoess, although Swede Nelson, Bob Kopf, and Tom Montgomery all would see playing time. Stoess was the chatterbox, the "Let's go, boys, let 'em have it" in the line. Chamberlain, who, like many of his teammates held elective student class and council positions, was another loud cheerleader on the field. The other players called him "Satch."

After two weeks the original eighty had been cut down to fifty, and Mr. Gloom conceded that with hard work and a few breaks they might make it through the season all right.

The beat writer for the *Trenton Evening Times* cut through Crisler's conservative outlook, predicting, "If Princeton doesn't go over the top this year, there are going to be a lot of people who miss their guesses."

That was not the kind of stuff Fritz Crisler wanted his team to be reading.

Everything about the preparation for the new football season at Yale was different from the past. The blending of coaches coming from different backgrounds was the least of the changes. It quickly became clear that things would be done according to the Greasy Neale method. There was no friction from Ducky Pond or the rest of the establishment.

Neale wanted the team to get away from the distractions of their classmates returning for the fall term. The Yale crew had a camp consisting of four small buildings at Gales Ferry, about sixty miles from New Haven on the Thames River, which it used as a base to train for the Harvard race in June. The football team would use it for ten days until classes started.

By September 3 the groundskeeper and equipment manager, William Perkins, had moved all the training equipment out of the Yale Armory and Lapham Field House to Gales Ferry. The boathouse would be used as a dressing room. The practice field, the field for the line machines, and the dummy tackling pits were ready.

In order to be at Gales Ferry on September 15, the first day they could practice, the players were asked to arrive two days earlier in New Haven for physical exams. There was no separate athletic dorm. Players had rooms scattered about the campus. Unless they were in the same classes, they didn't see much of each other away from the football field. Sophomores and seniors traveled in different circles.

Ducky Pond requested that a dorm be made available to them beginning September 13. But none of the rooms would be open for occupancy until the seventeenth. The administration balked over the cost and inconvenience of housing over seventy men in a dorm for a few days, then having them move into their regular rooms. Why, it could cost $200 or more for janitors and porters for those four days.

But Yale could afford it. Most of its games were played at home, as the Yale Bowl held a lot more people than most other eastern stadiums. Reserved seat ticket prices were considered steep for the times: $2.30 for the Columbia, Penn, Brown, and Georgia games; $3.10 for Dartmouth; $3.40 for Army; and $3.95 for Harvard—all plus ten cents for insured mailing. Visiting teams received one-third of the gross receipts, except for Harvard, which received 50 percent. In addition to gate receipts, the biggest revenue sources were sales of programs and season books and parking charges. The smallest source of income was the sale of used footballs, about a dozen a year, at $4 each.

Pond and Neale got their way.

The training table at Gales Ferry would cost $1,600 just to feed the squad for the ten days. Once school started, the players paid $10 a week for the training table dinners. That was more than the $7.50 other students paid for their meals, but they had a Swiss chef and the food was good, with plenty of steak and potatoes. The training table provided jobs for some members of the team as waiters; the other dining rooms used waitresses.

About seventy-five players reported. They were all walk-ons. The new ones with big prep school reputations were assigned to the freshman first team, but they had to perform to stay there.

Some of them might have been urged to go to Yale, but none was recruited in the sense of being wooed with perks, easy courses, tutors, or other more enticing lures. Some came from wealthy backgrounds and could afford it. Some, like Larry Kelley and Jimmy DeAngelis, had wealthy or club sponsors who paid their way. Some had to work. None of them went to Yale to play football; they went for the education and played football because they enjoyed it. A few belonged to one of the five exclusive senior secret societies, like Skull and Bones or Scroll and Key, each of which had only fifteen members.

Players, coaches, and training and kitchen staffs boarded buses for Gales Ferry at five o'clock on Friday, September 14. There were several notable absentees. Jerry Roscoe had an engagement at his home in San Diego and was given leave to report on Monday, after a seventeen-hour flight to New York. Junior end Bob Train, who had missed the '33 season on academic probation, sophomore tackle Meredith Scott, and junior back Dick Cummins were required to pass makeup exams in different subjects in order to be eligible to play. Senior Jimmy DeAngelis, expected to be a guard this year, also remained in New Haven to make up some classroom work.

That evening after dinner the coaches held a meeting. There would be two drills a day, at 9:30 and at 4:00, and blackboard lectures in between. They would trot the quarter mile to and from the field and the boathouse. Then the incoming captain, Clare Curtin, addressed them. Enthused by the new coaching setup, the usually easygoing Curtin had more fire and pep in his talk and his walk than his teammates were used to seeing in him. Yale teams had not been noted for their spirit and enthusiasm in recent years. Curtin was serving notice that this was about to change.

Yale teams were not known for their stamina. The difference between their condition and that of their main rivals, Harvard and Princeton, was often commented upon. Changing that was Major Wandle's job.

First thing every morning the major was out there barking orders in a military, not a "Yale," way. He went beyond the usual exercises. He had them stretching, going through discus-throwing motions—the forerunners of aerobics. Nobody complained; they couldn't because he was out in front of them, thirty years their senior, doing everything he asked of them right along with them.

Like many colleges, Yale had copied the Notre Dame box and line styles, with little success. The ND style of blocking used hands and arms. Columbia's upset of Stanford in the Rose Bowl inspired a new trend: linemen crouching low, blocking with the head and shoulders.

Neale switched the Bulldogs to the single wing, in which a guard or tackle might shift to the other side for an unbalanced line, and anyone in the backfield might shift into position to be a ball carrier or get the snap from the center. The defense would be a 6-2-2-1, the center and fullback up behind the line, then the running backs. The quarterback was the safety.

Practically all their time at Gales Ferry was devoted to fundamentals. They started in with two-a-day two-hour drills, concentrating on the arts of blocking and tackling more intensively than any of them had ever experienced, working on the 320-pound pyramid dummies. The ball had been made lighter and slimmer than ever, easier to handle. The first day they worked on passing and kicking formations.

Sundays were traditionally a day off. Not this year. Nobody minded. Had they sat down that day, they would have had two days of idleness; Monday it poured all day, and they were confined to indoor drills and lectures.

Given the widespread use of fake reverses and laterals, they drilled on watching the ball on defense, being aware of who had it. They practiced getting a quick start on the line. Officials would inquire of centers how they wanted the ball placed after each play: laces up, to the side, whatever. The rules allowed defensive linemen to start as soon as the center moved the ball, however slightly. They practiced getting that jump, over and over. They worked on trapping defenders, letting them come through the line, then sideswiping them. When they were trapped, Denny Myers taught them how to spin over on their back and get up and plug the hole. On offense, he taught the young tackles to coordinate with the man beside them on taking out a defender the play was going to go through.

One disconcerting aspect of the setup was the handful of spectators who watched from the perimeter of the practice field: a few old ladies, a young woman holding a baby, residents of the properties adjoining the field.

"Ducky would like to stage secret practice," Neale told a reporter, "but that's out when your field borders on people's property. We can't tell them to get out of their own backyards."

Concluding that none of the onlookers was a Harvard spy, they went about their business.

When everybody else was done for the day, Neale kept the centers and backs drilling on the snap. The center's job was much more demanding than it is today. He had to snap the ball to different backs in different locations at different speeds, depending on the play—high, low, leading the receiver right or left, right knee, right hip, etc. Neale would call out, "Right knee . . . waist high . . . lead left. . . ."

Jerry Roscoe arrived on Monday, Scott and Train on Wednesday, but it wasn't until Friday that Train learned he had passed his exam and could play. DeAngelis and Cummins also arrived on Friday in good standing. It would take until September 29 for Meredith Scott to be declared academically okay to play.

After ten days at Gales Ferry, Ducky Pond told AP football writer Louie Black, "I won't say we will be terrible, nor do I expect the team to be a world beater. There's nothing to do but try to plug along and do the best we can. . . . Whether the team will be strong enough to go through that schedule of ours successfully nobody knows. I wish I did."

They returned to New Haven tired but fit, feeling better prepared than they ever had, crammed with new ideas, ways to do things, upbeat. They had a better understanding of their new coaches. Greasy Neale was a detail man and the chief strategist, and they were impressed by him. They had come to appreciate and enjoy him, even though he was far from "the Yale breed." Neale was not the type who would have sworn to swear off swearing. He was himself and didn't try to be anything else. The captain, Clare Curtin, a quiet gentleman who never swore, said, "We were all fascinated by Greasy Neale. He was a colorful person. It was a great staff to work with."

Pond ordered the equipment from Gales Ferry installed at the freshman team's field instead of Anthony Thompson Field because they could hold secret workouts there.

Once classes began, they had practice every day from 3:00 to 6:00, with a night session maybe once a week. But practice never took precedence over the academic schedule. The first casualty was Chooch Train, who reinjured the shoulder he had hurt on the last day of spring practice.

Their scrimmages had more fire and drive than anyone could remember. They took on an aggressive, combative attitude so different from their "smilers" reputation of the past, the football expert of the *Times*, Allison Danzig, commented, "Yale football has gone elemental. The smoothie is out and caveman, roughened by a tough opening week of practice, has taken his place."

They had plenty of speed in the backfield but no elusiveness, no open-field threats like Princeton's Garry LeVan. Neale said,

"Once a back can shift for himself in a broken field, you can look for him to score if he gets past the line of scrimmage."

But Yale had no such weapons. The Bulldogs would have to fight their way past the goal line. "When you smell that goal line," Neale preached, "dive for it."

Timing and deception were the keys to the offense, a spin operation with a variety of options. The quarterback was the tailback in a formation right. Jerry Roscoe explained how it worked:

> The ball would come back to me. I would turn to spin and the fullback would come around and the wingback also, and I could hand off to either or keep it and run or pass or could shovel pass. I didn't run but enough to keep them honest. Sometimes the ball would go directly to the fullback and he could run with it. Sometimes the wingback would go out for a pass.
>
> After regular practice the coaches would have the center and backfield line up. They stood in a semicircle opposite us, and we would go through those procedures until the coaches couldn't tell who had the ball.

Roscoe and Neale got together every day for an hour or two before practice, going over play selection in different situations. Neale believed in starting a game conservatively. If Yale won the toss, he preferred to kick off, letting the other side deal with the pre-game nerves deep in its own territory before everybody had a few knocks and settled down.

Since the ball had been made slimmer for the '34 season, the passing game was enhanced. Neale worked with all the backs so that any one of them could throw a pass at the end of a trick play. The days of 3 yards and a cloud of dust were over, at least at Yale.

With the limited substitution rules, the coaches had to choose versatile linemen who could play different positions and backs who could not only run and pass and catch a pass but also block and tackle and kick. One of the casualties of those demands was the best punter at Gales Ferry, a six-foot-three, lean, left-footed kicker named Johnny Hersey. An end, he could boom 70-yarders down the field all day, but he couldn't break into the first team in the other departments. As a result he played only a few minutes and had to earn his glory as a Pulitzer Prize novelist.

In the end, only twenty-one players would see any significant action all season.

Early-season injuries and experiments in the shifting of linemen would give playing time to fullbacks Andrew Callan and Bob Schultz (the smallest on the squad at five-foot-six, 153 pounds), quarterback Ed King, halfback C. H. Buckley, and linemen John Overall, Charley Strauss, Richard Crampton, Dick Barr, and Webb Davis.

The Bulldogs had some talented players, but their ranks were thin. They lacked the depth of teams like Columbia, Army, Princeton, or Brown. And they knew it. They went into each game expecting to play until the end unless they were hurt or not doing the job, and they trained and prepared themselves accordingly. Nobody had to keep a close eye on them. They never broke training. They had to stay in shape knowing they would be expected to play as many minutes as they could every Saturday.

Given the team's lack of depth and exacting schedule, some experts questioned whether Yale would win a single game. One day Neale said to Pond, "If we could just use eleven men out there, we'd have a good team." By mid-season these were the men Neale would go with as his first string varsity:

Left end: Bob "Chooch" Train (anybody named "Train" was automatically dubbed Choo Choo or Chooch). Junior from Savannah, Georgia. Five-foot-eleven, 165 pounds. Fearless, cheerful, aggressive, intrepid, ran with a lope and never gave up on a play; ferocious swarming tackler. Meredith Scott called Train the best tackler on the team. "When he tackled, it was with arms and legs swarming like a cat leaping on a dog's back. He was all muscle and would fly through the air and grab a guy with arms and legs, maybe biting him too." An old shoulder injury limited his reach, so he was used more as a decoy than a pass receiver.

Left tackle: Meredith Scott. Sophomore from Gordonsville, Virginia. Six-foot-two-and-a-half, 195 pounds. The youngest at nineteen. Strong, dependable, would rapidly mature under fire.

Left guard: Francis Clare Curtin. Senior from North Abington, Massachusetts. Six-foot-one, 220 pounds. The heaviest lineman, stolid, quiet, immovable, inspiring respect as captain with dignity.

Center: Jimmy DeAngelis. Senior from New Haven. Five-foot-nine, 165 pounds. Dogged, dependable guard who was shifted around in the line and stymied by injuries; kind, considerate, amiable source of encouraging words on the line.

Right guard: Ben Grosscup. Senior from Charleston, West Virginia. Six feet, 175 pounds. Tough, cocky mountaineer given to swapping banter across the line.

Right tackle: Henry John "Jack" Wright. Sophomore from Bronxville, New York. Six-foot-one, 198 pounds. Dependable, solid plug in the defensive wall, good-natured, easygoing.

Right end: Larry Kelley. Sophomore from Williamsport, Pennsylvania. Six-foot-one, 185 pounds. Brash, lippy, agile pass receiver with big hands, quick and strong on defense; he had hurt his shoulder in high school and had nerve damage that bothered him, so he avoided head and shoulder contact by using a "pick-'em-up-and-throw-'em-down" tackling style. Kelley had a New York Yale Club scholarship and waited on tables for his board.

Quarterback: Jerome "Jerry" Roscoe. Junior from San Diego, California. Five-foot-eleven, 156 pounds. Steady, quiet, unflappable scholar and gentleman, not a scrambler, a line-drive passer with a quick release.

Halfback: Stratford "Strat" Morton. Senior from St. Louis, Missouri. Five-foot-nine, 158 pounds. Small-built, huge-hearted leader, the best all-around ball carrier, blocker, pass receiver, and tackler; covered his own ground and more backing up Kelley on defense; amiable, popular, ready with a joke to lighten things in the huddle.

Halfback: Bernard "Bernie" Rankin. Junior from Hyde Park, Massachusetts. Six feet, 182 pounds. Brilliant student, fastest broken-field runner on the team but didn't like the contact part of the game and "either couldn't or wouldn't tackle," said Bob Train. Neale would have to juggle playing Rankin for his running ability versus his defensive liabilities. On defense Rankin would line up behind Train because Chooch stopped everything that came his way, and Morton backed up Kelley, who had a tendency to roam to where he thought a play would go.

Fullback: Stan Fuller. Senior from Erie, Pennsylvania. Six feet, 175 pounds. The oldest at twenty-four, he had persevered through several prep schools and colleges to get accepted to Yale (or Princeton, which rejected him after he'd first been turned down by Yale), four years after graduating from high school. Some Erie people had paid his way to Roxbury Prep, where the coaches were all Yale men who persuaded him to keep plugging away until he could get into Yale. But financial inducements? Not at Yale. He would graduate with $1,200 in debts. Very quiet, unemotional, sound blocker and pass defender; shared punting duties with Whitehead.

Fullback: Mather "Kim" Whitehead. Junior from Bayside,

New York. Five-foot-eleven, 180 pounds. Fast, aggressive with amazing endurance; source of verbal back-patting during a game but normally taciturn, gruff, and dour-looking, so they called him "Happy."

8 | October 6

FRITZ CRISLER PRACTICED THE YO-YO METHOD OF PSYCHING up or down a team. Keeping a team that knows it's good from becoming overconfident can be just as tricky as getting a lesser team up for a game. It was good to knock his undefeated bunch a little, let them know that everybody was out to get them. His weekly routine was to take them down a notch on Monday, give them a few days to think about it, get tough on Thursday, and ease up on Friday. It was all charted, like the rest of Crisler's minutely detailed handwritten notes.

Crisler knew the importance of a well-stocked training table. By the time practice was over, there was nothing but stale meager leftovers at the eating halls and clubs. The team had its own dining room for meals after practice. This enabled Crisler to control the players' diets during the season. Unfortunately, when a case of food poisoning was served at the table, it meant that most of the team got sick. That's what happened ten days before the first game against Amherst. (The same thing happened to the Amherst team a few days later.) It set everything back a few days.

Then Garry LeVan tore up a knee in practice and would be out at least two weeks. Pepper Constable, who had hurt his back in the Yale game last year and sat out spring practice, was still bothered by it.

Films of other teams' games from last year were available but none from the current year. It was the scrubs' job to learn the next opponent's plays and run them against the first team. Amherst had won its first game, 22–0, over Connecticut State. Crisler hadn't scouted them. On Thursday, October 4, the scrubs ran Amherst plays from last year against the first-stringers. The Lord Jeffs had never beaten Princeton in nineteen games. Last year the Tigers had run over them, 40–0. They were the kind of cream puff opposition that prompted undergrads to circulate petitions for a tougher schedule.

For its part Amherst was content to do its best, take its licking, pick up its share of the gate, and go home in one piece. On Saturday the game was a skirmish, not a battle, a 75–0 track meet that proved nothing. All four Princeton squads saw playing time. Les Kaufman scored four touchdowns. But it came at a cost. Frank John, Pepper Constable, and Homer Spofford all suffered shoulder injuries during the brief time they played. There was a rumor that the team was so full of itself after the game, laughing and joking about the rout, that Crisler threatened to take them over to University Field and give them a real workout. Taking them down a notch in preparation for the next game had already begun.

(Amherst had had enough of playing warm-up doormat to Princeton and asked to be excused for 1935. Princeton replaced it with Navy.)

Greasy Neale was intrigued by Columbia's KF-79 play, on which Al Barabas had scored to beat Stanford in the Rose Bowl. Never hesitant about borrowing what worked for others, Neale ordered a print of the newsreel film that showed the play. He wanted to study it frame by frame to see what every player was doing every second. The only way he could do that was by holding it over a light with a magnifier. What he saw was a counterplay. Columbia pulled a lineman to the right side for a power play. The quarterback turned his back to the line, faked to the fullback, and handed off to Barabas, who went around the weak side behind his interference.

Neale added his own variations to it, saying, "We didn't take their play. We improved on it." The Bulldogs also practiced defending it in case Columbia used it in the opener against Yale on October 6.

All week they worked on what the coaches considered glaring weaknesses in the fundamentals of blocking and tackling.

The entire backfield remained a puzzle. Tom Curtin had been bothered by a tender ankle since Gales Ferry. The line was unsettled. DeAngelis, a guard last year, was tried at center and end. One day the timing drills were going so poorly that Neale switched the entire first and second teams. Another day the varsity looked its sharpest, reeling off four touchdowns against the scrubs. Tom Curtin drop-kicked two extra points.

By Friday they had a starting lineup, but they still didn't know what they had. Only one of the sophomores, Meredith Scott, started. In the first game they would use twenty-one men, including three quarterbacks and twelve linemen—the most they would use in a game all year.

Saturday morning it rained heavily until noon and drizzled through the first half. It was warm, humid, muggy. The equipment manager, a Spalding employee they called "Hokus" who was stationed at Yale for the season, handed out the brand-new dark blue wool jerseys and khaki pants. On each arm of the jerseys were two patches of rubberized material to help in holding and catching the ball, one four-by-nine on the upper arm and one four-by-six on each forearm. In the middle of the jersey, rising to a point, were five vertical strips of the same material, each about two inches wide. The heavy jerseys weighed about two pounds. All the padding was built in; a ten-inch patch of felt four inches wide went down the back of each arm. Each jersey had a number on the back. The pants, made out of a canvas called airplane cloth, came down just below the knees. Hip and thigh pads were a combination of felt and fiberboard. Small leather shoulder pads were felt lined.

The helmets were a stiff but flexible leather with a reinforcing rawhide around the sides and a small webbing inside on top. They were held on with a string tied under the chin. It was not uncommon to see a player walking down Main Street to practice with the ear flaps turned up and tied together with the string on top of his head.

The student manager, Francis "Pat" Garvan, was busy seeing that all the pre-game preparations were in order. Garvan was in charge of transportation for away games in addition to dressing room needs, and he oversaw the assistant student managers. One was assigned to assist visiting teams if anything was needed, a courtesy not extended at all schools. Lou Walker drew that assignment for the Columbia game. Another one took orders from Major Wandle, seeing to the cart supplies, water buckets, towels—whatever Wandle wanted done.

Wandle taped every man's ankles two hours before the 2:00 p.m. kickoff to allow time for the tape to stretch. This was a weekly ritual. For some reason, that day he ordered all the players rubbed down with hot oil and liniment before they put on the heavy wool jerseys. Meredith Scott said, "About five minutes into the game, the huddle looked like a volcano. We were sweating inside the helmets. You could see the steam coming out of everybody. At halftime they had to rub us off with alcohol and [we had to] change into lighter jerseys for us to survive."

The rain kept the crowd down to about twenty-two thousand. Just before the kickoff, the starters huddled, held hands, and Clare Curtin said, "Let's go get 'em."

From start to finish, it was a hard-fought, grinding contest with all the stops pulled out. But for most of the game Yale could do nothing to contain the Rose Bowl hero, Al Barabas. Built like a prototype for a Sherman tank, Barabas was the main factor in Columbia's outrushing Yale, 352–53. That the Bulldogs held him to two touchdowns and a 12–6 score was a tribute to their unflagging determination.

In the first quarter Barabas broke through the left side as two Lions blocked off Scott. Tom Curtin made Greasy Neale wince as he misplayed his chance to tackle Barabas, who went 70 yards into the end zone untouched. In the third quarter he scored again after a 75-yard drive full of fake spinners and fake reverses.

Clare Curtin played only twenty-five minutes and became ill.

For young Scott, it was a painful introduction to big-time college football: "The Columbia right end, Harry Chase, was making a monkey out of me. I'd never run into a head block before. I was used to grabbing the end and pushing him by and going across the line. He was using his head, not his shoulder. I was bigger than he was, but it's effective if you're not looking for it. The first time it got me right in the breadbasket. He did that about three times before I caught on to what was happening. Then he mousetrapped me on a play in the third quarter. I went through the line and got kicked in the face and got a nosebleed and was yanked."

Sophomore Jack Wright replaced Scott and finished the game.

Late in the third quarter Strat Morton and Larry Kelley went in; Roscoe took over at quarterback and led a drive, running and passing to Train and Overall, capping the drive with a pass to Kelley in the left corner of the end zone.

They showed no quit. With a few minutes to play, Columbia reached the goal line again. This time Callan, Morton, and Overall stopped Barabas cold. From deep in his end zone Roscoe threw two long passes. The first was almost caught by Morton, who fell just short of reaching the ball. The second fell incomplete as the game ended.

Yale's ground game had been stymied, but the passing attack had shown more flair and imagination than the Yale Bowl had ever seen. One new play came out of a kick formation, with a wingback having the option to throw to one of three scattered receivers.

Yale followers were not used to this brand of tenacious, wide open football. They stood and cheered the new Blue look, even as Columbia rooters razed the goalposts.

9 | October 13

CAL RIPKEN SR., LONGTIME BALTIMORE ORIOLES COACH, believed, "Practice doesn't make perfect. Perfect practice makes perfect. If you practice sloppy, you'll play sloppy."

In the week following the Amherst picnic, the Tigers didn't take things seriously. Although the Williams starting line was big, averaging 200 pounds, it would never be able to withstand the two or three armies that Crisler could throw at it on October 13. Anticipating another track meet, the Tigers fooled around in practice. Crisler came up with two or three new plays for each game. They thought it would be fun to create a few fancy new plays of their own. No matter what he said, Crisler just couldn't puncture that cocky balloon.

So behind the dour expression he wore sitting on the bench that Saturday, Crisler might have been secretly pleased when the Williams defense stubbornly stopped his powerful offensive machine until early in the second period. Princeton led 14–0 at halftime.

Ken Sandbach took the second-half kickoff 90 yards for a touchdown. Crisler, who seemed to be able to follow what every man on the field was doing on every play, later pointed out that it wasn't Sandbach's running but the precise blocking by five other men that made it possible.

Crisler had three complete teams he could run out there to wear down the scrappy but outmanned Williams forces. The line, which Crisler admitted might not be as bad as he had feared, shut them down. Williams scored on a pass in the final minutes to make it 35–6.

But Crisler was disturbed by his team's tendency to fumble and drop passes. They completed only 8 of 20 passes and fumbled 3 times, losing the ball each time.

Yale came out of the Columbia game with its line in even more disarray. Jimmy DeAngelis strained a back muscle. He would re-injure it in the first five minutes against Penn on October 13 and be out for three weeks. Wright replaced Scott in practice. Charley Strauss, a sophomore guard, was plugged into the tackle slot. Clare Curtin rested a lame ankle for a few days.

In the Columbia game, Ben Grosscup had missed a block and fallen on the Lions' star tackle, Paul Jackel, breaking Jackel's leg and ending his season. Line coach Denny Myers took that as a sign of Grosscup's willingness to maim opponents. He picked out a target in the Penn lineup and told Grosscup, "I want you to get this guy."

But that wasn't Grosscup's style. The injury to Jackel had been an accident. Grosscup ignored the suggestion, but as much as he valued what he had learned from Myers, the incident lowered his opinion of the coach.

The week began with blackboard talks and signal drills. In the next two days' scrimmages against the scrubs, using Penn plays and defenses, they looked sluggish. During one scrimmage, Roscoe wrenched his shoulder and hip while making a tackle. His status was uncertain for Saturday.

The Bulldogs pulled themselves together and managed to get by a mistake-prone Penn team populated primarily by sophomores, 14–6, on a cold, windy afternoon. But they didn't look impressive doing it. In the first two minutes Strat Morton ran 61 yards to score. Extra-point efforts were usually dropkicks or placekicks. Clare Curtin used the placekick to make it 7–0. For the rest of the half the heavy Penn line plugged up the Yale ground game, while Penn threatened several times, twice fumbling inside the Yale 20—they fumbled 7 times—to stall drives.

In the third quarter the Elis got another break when a Penn punt blew out of bounds at the Penn 22. A pass to Kelley set up a 9-yard end run by Roscoe, and it was 14–0.

Penn then used a pulverizing ground game, tearing through the line in grinding out six first downs, covering 75 yards for a touchdown. Joe Johnson, the third center used by Yale, intercepted two passes to stop other Penn efforts.

When Dick Barr aggravated an old knee injury (the knee had been operated on after last season), the crowd enjoyed an amusing pantomime on the field.

The athletic and health departments at Yale had instituted a new policy concerning the use of stretchers to remove an injured player from the field. Game programs contained the following note: "Attention is called to the fact that all players receiving joint injuries of the lower extremities and certain other injuries are removed from the field on a stretcher. This is true even in the case of minor injuries and should cause no alarm to the player's family and friends."

When Major Wandle saw Dick Barr limping after a play, he rolled out the stretcher. The tall, portly major tried to assist Barr onto the gurney. Barr refused to oblige. After an animated discussion, seen but unheard by the crowd, Barr limped off alongside the stretcher as the crowd cheered.

Otherwise there was little to cheer about. It was not a glorious afternoon. The Roscoe aerial circus was limited to 3 completions out of 6 attempts. Yale had gotten a few breaks and needed them. The defense had been much too porous. The middle of the line was still unsettled. Now DeAngelis had a bad back and Barr and Whitehead had knee injuries. Joe Johnson was discovered to have a broken bone in his wrist.

"We have a long way to go," said Ducky Pond.

10 | October 20

ON MONDAY, OCTOBER 15, FORTY WRITERS GATHERED AT Osborn Field House for their annual in-depth press conference with the football coaches. Mr. Gloom was in good form. We beat Williams, he told them, only because our second- and third-stringers were better than theirs. They had used thirty-three men. "I don't believe that if we had to play eleven men against eleven all afternoon we would have had an easy time of it at all." Our play has been spotty, he said, full of mistakes, "and all that fumbling might be disastrous against a stronger opponent."

Crisler still felt the loss of tackles Ceppi and Lane and end Ken Fairman. His sophomores were not as good as last year's sophs. He defended Princeton's schedule—"Don't let anyone tell you that Princeton isn't facing the hardest sort of work against plenty of opponents before the end of the year"—and saw "nothing but trouble lying ahead," beginning with the Washington and Lee Generals, who were coming to town gunning for them.

The Generals had their entire backfield from last year, including their sensational lefty passer, Bill Seaton. They had been brooding for a year over what they thought was a victory unjustly taken from them by officials' rulings. They were looking for vengeance. The Tiger was out to put them in their place. After three wins so far, W&L had lost to West Virginia, 12–0, on an interception and blocked kick. Crisler sent freshman coach Ken Fairman to scout them.

When Crisler said he never knew until five minutes before a game who his starters would be, he was not just being coy. LeVan was healing but still stiff-legged. Spofford was still out. Sandbach and Constable had bruised shoulders. Constable had insisted on scrimmaging all week and went to his room hurting worse each night as the week went on. The light pads the players wore, unlike the armor of today, were slim protection against the beating the shoulders took in tackling and being tackled.

Before the game Earl Martineau gave out the names of the players who would dress for the game. Constable, LeVan, and Sandbach were not on it. Ippy Ruton-Miller would start at fullback and Les Kaufman and Paul Pauk at halfback.

Fritz Crisler was sitting alone in a small room off the dressing room. Martineau came in. Crisler said he'd been thinking; it might be a good idea to have Constable, LeVan, and Sandbach in uniform on the bench "just in case."

All week Fritz Crisler had harped on how tough the Generals would be to defeat. But he didn't imagine they would be this tough. Neither did the twenty-seven thousand spectators who were in for a nonstop frenzy of excitement.

The Generals came out full of fury, like bulls in a rodeo, and outplayed and outsmarted the Orange and Black for most of the first half. They scored early in the first quarter on a 38-yard pass that had the secondary so fooled they could make only a half-hearted attempt to tackle the receiver. It was the first points scored against the Princeton first-string team since 1932. Hugh MacMillan blocked the extra-point kick.

W&L kept the Tigers bottled up deep in their own territory for the entire first quarter. Three times within five minutes Mac-Millan had to punt from behind his goal line with a fierce wave of Generals bearing down on him. Mac had no chance to win the kicking game that day over W&L's Bill Ellis.

How they kept the Generals from scoring more often is a tribute to the Princeton line. Afterward Crisler admitted that he had no more worries about his tackles. His line, he said, was a whole lot better than he had expected.

Early in the game Ruton-Miller was kicked in the head and had to leave. Like the shoulder pads, the soft, pliable leather helmets with no face masks were a puny safeguard compared to the modern uncrackable head safes. Crisler sent in the sore-shouldered Pepper Constable. When Ruton-Miller returned to the game and took another hit in the head, Constable went back in.

Quarterback Katz Kadlic was also hurt twice and had to come out each time, but he wound up finishing the game. Trying to get the stalled offense rolling, Crisler sent in Sandbach. Late in the second quarter Kadlic took to the air. Two passes to MacMillan and a lateral to Jim Miller, in for Kaufman, took the Tigers to the 21. Sandbach and Constable carried them to the 14. Then Kadlic passed to Lea for the tying touchdown. Sandbach kicked the extra point to make it 7–6 at the half.

Throughout the first half Fritz Crisler sat scowling. Press box observers who were familiar with that "black look" didn't know exactly what he would say at halftime, but they knew whatever it was, it would be eloquent.

Whatever he said must have worked; the Tigers came out like a different team and marched down the field. But there was nothing different about one chronic weakness: fumbleitis. Three times they were in high gear on a scoring drive, and each time they fumbled it away.

W&L played them tough all the way. With nine minutes to play, the Generals were on their own 47. Four plays later—three of them passes—they scored again. The kick was wide. W&L led 12–7.

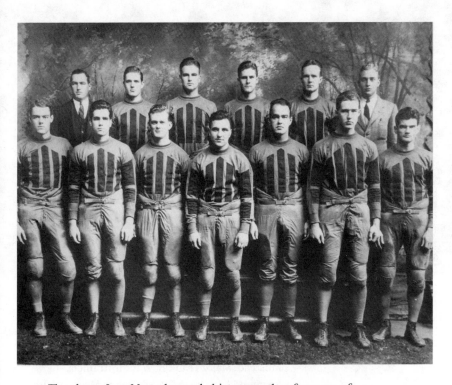

The eleven Iron Men who made history on the afternoon of November 17, 1934, not only by handing Princeton its only defeat in three years, but also as the last eleven to play the entire sixty minutes in a major college football game. Front row, from left: Larry Kelley, Jack Wright, Ben Grosscup, Jimmy DeAngelis, Clare Curtin, Meredith Scott, Bob Train. Back row, from left: Coach Raymond W. "Ducky" Pond, Strat Morton, Kim Whitehead, Jerry Roscoe, Stan Fuller, manager Pat Garvan.

(*Above*) The 1934 Yale coaching staff, from left: Earle "Greasy" Neale, Stewart P. Scott, Century Milstead, Major Frank A. Wandle (trainer), Raymond W. "Ducky" Pond, Denny Myers, Walter Levering, Ivan Williamson.

(*Opposite top*) Yale assistant coach Earle "Greasy" Neale. Neale played in the 1919 World Series with the Cincinnati Reds and went on to a place in the Pro Football Hall of Fame as the coach of the Philadelphia Eagles.

(*Opposite bottom*) Larry Kelley in a familiar role: pursued in vain by a horde of defenders after catching a pass from Jerry Roscoe.

To Adelaide.
With good
wishes and
all the luck
in this world.
Earle Jersey Meale

The 1934 Yale football team. Front row, from left: Webb Davis, Strat Morton, Stan Fuller, Bernie Rankin, Clare Curtin, Jerry Roscoe, Tom Curtin, Ben Grosscup, Larry Kelley. Second row: Jack Wright, Meredith Scott, Webster Bull, Meffert, Richard Crampton, Jimmy DeAngelis, Sidney Towle, Edward King, Andrew Callan, John Hersey, Richard Cummins. Back row: Bob Train, Carter Higgins, Richard Barr, Charles Strauss, John Runnals, John Edmonds, Joseph Johnson, Malcolm Watson, Fred Stewart, Richard Herold, Robert Schultz, John Overall.

Fortieth reunion. Only Strat Morton, killed in a military plane crash during World War II, failed to make it to the fortieth Iron Men reunion. Front row, from left: Larry Kelley, Jack Wright, Ben Grosscup, Jimmy DeAngelis, Clare Curtin, Meredith Scott, Bob Train. Back row, from left: Kim Whitehead, Jerry Roscoe, Stan Fuller.

Sixtieth reunion. Five Iron Men were feted at their sixtieth reunion in 1994. Standing from left: Larry Kelley, Jimmy DeAngelis, Meredith Scott, Jerry Roscoe; seated: Kim Whitehead.

Crisler read the posture of his players on the field. They were tired. They looked down, ready to be counted out. They needed a lift. The crowd roared when they saw Garry LeVan get off the bench and trot, a little stiff-legged, onto the field, replacing Sandbach. You could almost hear the bugle call of the cavalry coming to the rescue of the beleaguered wagon train.

With time running out, LeVan returned a punt 15 yards to midfield. Kadlic passed to Lea incomplete, but interference was called at the 23. LeVan came out of the backfield and went up in the air with two Generals fighting for a high throw from Kadlic. LeVan came down with it on the 2-yard line. Then it was LeVan through the line to within a foot of the goal line. They gave the ball to the pile driver, Constable, who went through for the score. MacMillan's kick was good, and it was 14–12.

The game ended a minute later when Les Kaufman intercepted a pass on his 30 and ran it 69 yards behind a wall of blockers before being forced out of bounds just shy of a touchdown.

Both teams earned a cloak of glory. W&L had played well enough to win. Princeton had demonstrated that it had what it took to overcome a poor first half and come back like a champion.

On Sunday evening, standing in front of the fireplace at Osborn Field House, Fritz Crisler said, "The most satisfying thing I learned yesterday is that the Princeton team is capable of courageous and brilliant playing when it is the underdog. In this first major test I was able to tell that our line shows promise of being as good defensively as you could expect it to be. Dave Chamberlain, George Stoess, and Swede Nelson are doing well at the tackle positions." He concluded, "I'm very glad the Washington and Lee game is over."

Allison Danzig of the *New York Times* wrote, "The game must have been a big shock to everyone at Princeton. The chances are, however, that it will be the making of the Tiger for the tests ahead and rid the camp of any semblance of the overconfidence which Fritz Crisler has been striving to guard against. W&L deserves all credit for its game fight against odds, and will probably receive the thanks of the Princeton coaching staff if Nassau hurdles its remaining objectives. Right now it looks as though Yale will be the team that the Tiger will have to reckon with most seriously."

Columnist John Kieran commented, "Yale's chances against Princeton in the annual collision now look much brighter than they did a week ago."

Ducky Pond couldn't see that far ahead. Sitting in his office in Ray Tompkins House before practice to prepare for the upcoming game against Brown, he said, "So far we've been able to go out and get a touchdown now and then when the chance presented itself, but the other fellows have wandered through far too much. Penn at times made a parade of it. No use scouting unless you can stop the other fellow."

After a light Monday workout, the Bulldogs had worked on the passing game without Roscoe and drilled against Brown plays for two hours in a secret session that left Pond dissatisfied. Scrubs coach Stewart Scott had scouted Brown and prepared his men well to test the first string in scrimmages. They ran through the tackles for long gains. The downfield tackling was lackluster.

By Wednesday's session the atmosphere was entirely different. It was as if all the starters realized not only that they were better than they had shown against Penn, but that they *had* to be better to survive what lay ahead. It was a session unlike any that habitual onlookers could recall.

It began with a dummy scrimmage against the scrubs, the coaches halting plays to point out mistakes. Pond, barking through a small megaphone hanging on a cord around his neck, and Neale, who didn't need one, harped over and over on quick starts in the line: "Quick start. . . quick start . . . drive . . . drive . . . start . . . start . . . watch the ball . . . who's got the ball . . . follow the ball. . . ." Then they went into a real scrimmage against Brown plays. The air over Anthony Thompson Field rang with the voices of the players shouting to each other, calling out words of encouragement. The thuds and grunts of blocks and tackles mixed with the coaches' calls to watch the ball, drive, drive, start, start. . . .

It got dark. The arc lights were turned on, and Major Wandle produced a ball painted white. They moved to the varsity 10-yard line, where the scrubs attacked the tackles and tore through the line. Plays were stopped, adjustments made.

The workout was long and exhausting but spirited to the end. Fortunately there were no injuries.

The juggling act continued. The three veteran centers—DeAngelis, Barr, and Johnson—all seniors, were sidelined. Ben Grosscup, who had played end, guard, and center at Choate and Yale, was moved to center. Webb Davis would start at left guard, Charley Strauss at right guard. In the backfield, Bernie Rankin was promoted from the second team to a halfback position with Strat Morton. Whitehead, who had been bouncing from one backfield post to another, was set at fullback, Roscoe at quarterback. It was the first time that backfield alignment would start together.

The Bulldogs took that caveman spirit into the Yale Bowl on Saturday and carried out an impressive, unexpected 37–0 rout of a good Brown team that had won two games and was rated an even-money bet. Every facet of the Elis' game was executed perfectly. Their outweighed line got those quick, driving starts and beat their opponents both ways. Roscoe saw a wide open defense and put Greasy Neale's aerial innovations into play, and Brown never adjusted. He completed 9 of 14 passes for two touchdowns, throwing to Kelley and Whitehead going down and out on the right side and Morton cutting across the middle from right halfback. A new play featuring some dazzling who's-got-the-ball sleight-of-hand culminated in a Roscoe to Morton pass good for 61 yards. Kim Whitehead scored three times, once on an interception. Kelley scored twice, once on a kick blocked by Scott that bounded up in the air right into Kelley's hands. Rankin took a long lateral from Morton and ran around right end for a touchdown.

With a 31–0 lead at halftime, most of the first team got some rest. Only Ben Grosscup, with no backups at center, put in as much as fifty-seven minutes. It would be the only time all season that so many men would have a chance to come off the bench and see some action. One of them was Johnny Hersey, who went in at left end for John Overall.

Greasy Neale was not surprised by the turnaround from the week before, or even from one day's practice to the next. Like all veteran college coaches, he knew he was dealing with young men, subject to the pressures of classwork, grades, financial problems, girlfriends, family situations, maybe something they ate one day—all the usual challenges and mysteries of maturing. One day they might look poor in practice and the next day—well, like they had looked on Wednesday.

For the same reasons, they were never the same team from one week to the next. Neither were their opponents, for that matter, making the predicting of winners a hazardous occupation.

One thing the veteran scouts at the Yale Bowl that afternoon agreed on: this Yale team had more spirit than any Yale team of the past ten years.

11 | October 27

<small>RUSH WEEK, KNOWN AS CLUB BICKER WEEK, BEGAN ON MON-</small>day on the Nassau campus. Sophomores were rushed by the exclusive upper-class eating clubs, a much-sought honor. Football players were high on the clubs' lists. The rushing, especially by veteran members of the football team toward their sophomore teammates, disrupted practice. Crisler could not abide distractions, not during practice, not the day of a game, not during the few trips to away games. He didn't want to hear any talk about eating clubs, girls, post-game dates—nothing but football.

To get the players away from the campus, on Wednesday he announced that they'd be taken by bus after practice every day and spend the night at Princeton Prep for the rest of the week. They'd be returned each morning in time for classes.

The effectiveness of the W&L passing game caused Crisler to concentrate on strengthening the pass defense. That and further drilling on fundamentals would occupy the week's preparation for Cornell. The Ithacans had a thin squad and hadn't beaten Princeton since 1928, but Crisler refused to take them lightly. Coach Net Poe taught the scrubs the Cornell plays, and they scrimmaged so intently Dave Chamberlain took a blow that broke a tooth and wrenched his jaw. Ippy Ruton-Miller was in the infirmary with an eye infection.

But Garry LeVan was healthy, and he and MacMillan excelled at booming 50-yard punts all week.

In a Friday interview a seemingly relaxed Fritz the Reticent was in good form. Asked if he had anything to say about the game or his team's condition, he said, "Yes. We will be in Palmer Stadium at two o'clock tomorrow for the opening kickoff."

In a steady rain the Princeton team nearly achieved the impossible: satisfying their coach. Everything worked according to

Crisler's blueprint. The Tiger gained the momentum early, and the new plays clicked. On almost every play of the first quarter MacMillan lined up in punt formation and seldom punted. He ran, passed, or pulled off reverses and fakes with precision. In the first minute of play he threw a short pass to Sandbach, who took it 47 yards for a touchdown.

From a short kick formation, Sandbach threw to LeVan on the sideline, who snaked his way behind solid blocking for a 65-yard touchdown, then took the rest of the day off. Paul Pauk came in and produced as much firepower with his speed as any first-string back. The Tiger simply had too many weapons for Cornell and fired them all with precision. Everything was executed flawlessly with a teamwork not seen in two years. The line held like a wall, twice on goal-line stands.

The 45–0 final score was the highest Princeton had run up against Cornell since a 46–0 romp in 1893.

The Army team had started the season as an unknown quantity. It had lost eight starters to graduation and had a new head coach. But as usual it was fortified by transfers from other schools. (Princeton refused to play Army because it disagreed with the lax eligibility rules at West Point. Men who had played at other colleges before gaining appointments to the academy were allowed to play immediately. Similar transfers to Yale or Princeton had to sit out a year.) After four games Army had rolled up 138 points and had yet to give up a point. It was coming off a 48–0 wrecking of a Drake team that had been expected to be trouble. Army, listed as a 5–3 favorite, hadn't lost to Yale since 1929.

"If Yale can beat Army Saturday," said a wire service story, "Pond will be hailed as a 'miracle man' because he took over a team that appeared physically inadequate to face its tough schedule and a squad that seemed entirely too small."

Like any successful coach, Ducky Pond didn't let his men coast on their impressive defeat of Brown. Monday afternoon he spent an hour lecturing them about the mistakes they had made. For the next few days they worked until long after dark, scrimmaging against Army plays. Morton, Rankin, and Kelley were cutting through the scrubs' replicated Army defense for long gains. They practiced Greasy Neale's newest innovations. One of them, which they would run against Army, may have been illegal. The play was a screen pass to a receiver a few feet past the line. Linemen immediately formed a screen of interference in front of him. The rule said, "When ineligible players who have crossed the line of scrimmage in any way obstruct the right of way of an opponent on a forward pass which has crossed the line of scrimmage, it is interference."

Army captain Joe Stancook would claim interference on the play, but the officials didn't call it.

Neither team was able to work out in Yale Bowl on Friday; it was protected from a driving rain and howling wind by a heavy tarp purchased several years earlier from former Philadelphia Athletics pitcher Howard Ehmke, who had gone into the tarp business while still an active player. Nevertheless, the Elis drilled outside on Thompson Field. The Cadets worked out in Coxe Field House.

The wind blew the rain away on Saturday, and a full Bowl was expected for the first time that fall. New Haven authorities announced that automobile traffic would not be directed away from downtown. Visitors would be welcome to enjoy lunch there before going to the game.

At 1:15 the cadets marched into the Bowl, always a stirring sight. By kickoff there were forty-five thousand spectators.

Breaks figured in all the day's scoring.

Army won the toss, elected to kick off, and quickly reaped the benefit. Rankin caught it at the 6 and followed his planned interference for 30 yards when two cadets got to him and jarred the ball loose and fell on it. Five plays later Army led 7–0.

In the second quarter Jack Buckler was back to punt for Army. Bob Train raced in, leaped in the air, and partially blocked it. Buckler fell to the ground, one knee sticking up. Train landed on it, right in the gut. It knocked the wind out of him. He lay on the ground retching with dry heaves but didn't want to come out. Clare Curtin waved off a substitute, but still Train couldn't get up. When the officials wouldn't hold up the game any longer, Major Wandle rolled out the stretcher and took him off.

Spectators were urged to not assume a serious injury had occurred just because a stretcher was used. But to radio audiences, just the mention of the stretcher created images of serious damage.

"My mother and father were listening to the game in Savannah," Train recalled, "and when they heard Ted Husing say I was being carried off on a stretcher, they burned up the wires calling New Haven. I was all right but they never let me back in the game."

Shortly after Overall replaced Train, he missed a block, and the Army end smothered Whitehead's kick on the Yale 3. Two plays later it was 14–0.

Yale came back when a long punt by Fuller was downed by Overall on the Army 15 and possession was given to Yale, reportedly because of a clipping penalty against Army. On the first play Rankin ran it in to make it 14–6.

The entire third period was played in Yale's backyard, the Cadets banging their way through the line, the Bulldogs stalling the attack each time until finally giving way at the end of the quarter. It was now 20–6.

The Elis weren't finished. Roscoe went to the air: on a 40-yard pass to Kelley, interference was called against Army. A pass to Fuller took them to the 24. A pass to Kelley on a down-and-out pattern was caught at the 14, and Kelley raced down the sideline.

"I was nearing the goal line," Kelley said, "and I smelled it and dove for it like Neale preached to us and Jack Buckler nearly broke my back. He was coming across, and as I was stretched out diving, he hit me and knocked me out of bounds at the 3-yard line."

Bernie Rankin carried it in to make it 20–12.

The Cadets were on the march again when the game ended.

Seven Yale men—Grosscup, Curtin, Kelley, Strauss, Morton, Rankin, and Roscoe—played all sixty minutes. Army's quick early strike never got them down. Lacking the powerhouse punch of a Stancook and Buckler, they had used resourcefulness and grit to match the Cadets on the scoreboard the rest of the game, except for Curtin's missed extra points, one of which was blocked.

Both teams had played hard, intelligent football. When Army backs broke through the line, the Yale backfield was right on them with fierce tackling. Roscoe completed 9 passes for 114 yards to Army's 36 in the air. Jack Buckler's punts gained on balance against those of Whitehead, but Fuller more than matched him when Whitehead came out with a sprained ankle.

In the end the Army line made the difference. It held Yale to 88 yards rushing to Army's 222. The Cadets did it partly with light, polite, bantering. Nothing nasty, no trash talk, just distracting chatter: "Hey, is that Grosscup over there? Let's take a crack at him." Or, "There's Captain Curtin. Hello, Clare."

There was some intimidation too. In the third quarter Meredith Scott replaced Jack Wright at left tackle. He took his position and looked across the line directly at the Army right guard, Robert Stillman. Stillman had played for two years at Colorado College before gaining entrance to West Point. He was twenty-three; Scott was nineteen. "He looked old enough to be my father," Scott said. "I felt like I ought to be saying good afternoon, sir. He hadn't shaved for a few days and he had a black jowl. I stared at it; I was just starting to shave myself. He weighed about 230 and looked as big as a mountain. I came out of that game pretty hard-bitten. Nobody fazed me after that."

Larry Kelley admitted, "We were a little outmanned." The ends took a beating. "The thin leather helmets had only one earhole," Kelley said. "On defense the tackles could use their hands and slapped the ends on the head. Another tactic was the forearm shiver—two straight-arms to the face." Kelley wound up with two broken eardrums that would keep him out of the armed forces.

John Kieran observed that "Yale's determination in the face of a powerful Army attack is helping to set the stage for a brisk November battle between the Tiger and the Bulldog."

12 | November 3

PRINCETON AND HARVARD HAD NOT MET ON THE FOOTBALL field since 1926, a Princeton win at Cambridge that was marked by accusations that the home team wore signet rings used as brass knuckles. A fist fight broke out around the goal posts after the game. Campus publications fired insults and belittling cartoons at each other. Princeton had also taken umbrage when Harvard administrators decided there was nothing sacred about their rivalry. Henceforth they would go outside their eastern bias and schedule Michigan in place of Princeton. So they broke up.

Students petitioned at both schools to renew the rivalry until 1933, when, faced with the need for more revenue in lean times, the value of a reliable gate attraction outweighed the luxury of an old pout. The schools agreed to meet again starting this year. They figured to draw about forty-five thousand to the thirty-one-year-old Harvard Stadium, the oldest football stadium in the country. Both sides promised to leave all signet rings at home. Marching bands would salute each other's followers. The two teams would get together for a friendship dinner—no speeches—after the game at Lowell House.

Fritz Crisler was actually a little cheerful before heading to Cambridge on Friday, November 2. Homer Spofford and Ippy Ruton-Miller were the only players out of action, though Kadlic and Constable still ached across the shoulders. His team was a three-touchdown favorite, and Crisler didn't even argue with that assessment. But arriving in Cambridge, he dropped the smile and declared that he looked forward to "the hardest sort of encounter."

Some Harvard students questioned all the hoopla surrounding a football game at a time of long breadlines and tar paper shack communities. During the game they held up signs: WHO CARES?

The game was polite. There was one unnecessary roughness penalty against Harvard. The Tiger scored three touchdowns and won, 19–0, but they blew five other opportunities to score, with three fumbles and two dropped passes at the goal line. It seemed as if they had to be pushed to be at their best.

After the game Crisler praised Harvard's fighting spirit. Ignoring the near-loss to Washington and Lee, he built up his team with some exaggeration by saying it "met the sternest test it has been asked to face this season and I am proud as are all of us of the way it met that test." There would be time enough on Monday to point out mistakes and take his Tigers down a peg. He called it a great game, but the fact was Harvard's line—six of whom played the entire game—gallant though it was, couldn't hold off the inexhaustible mine of replacement forces at Crisler's disposal.

Dartmouth had never won in the Yale Bowl. It was 0-16 over the past fifty years. This year it believed it was due. Last year's freshman team had beaten the Yale frosh for the first time ever. Five of those freshmen were now on the varsity. Dartmouth was undefeated in five games, outscoring its opponents 135–0. Its schedule included some lightweights, but everybody's dance card except Yale's had some waltzes. Coach Earl Blaik could send in fresh legs at any time, rotating six halfbacks of equal ability. Like Fritz Crisler, he could substitute an entire team if he wanted to.

For the second week in a row Yale would face a team that had not been scored upon.

By now both teams had scouted each other enough to know what to expect. Blaik was of the "keep it simple" school of football. He was not likely to spring any new tricks. Greasy Neale never stopped inventing. This week they would work on variations of the shovel or flip pass and the lateral to improve their running game, in light dummy scrimmages without helmets.

But Neale couldn't invent anything to heal his ailing linemen. They had no healthy centers. During the week they experimented, moving Grosscup from tackle to center, Curtin from tackle to guard. Johnny Hersey, an end, was tried at a guard slot.

With Kim Whitehead unlikely to play, Neale turned his attention to Stan Fuller. On Monday he said, "Fuller, our scouting reports are that Dartmouth doesn't pass much. I want you to play up close back of the line. You're not going to be responsible for breaking up any pass plays. All I want you to do is make the tackles. We're going to have a seven-man line and diamond defense. They have a running guard who leads all the plays. Wherever that guard goes, you go. Meet him coming through the hole and if you can knock him down and get the tackle, good. But bang up that hole."

Stan Fuller did everything Neale had asked of him as Yale outplayed Dartmouth in the first half, rolling up ten first downs

to three. Dartmouth reached the Yale 13 in the first three minutes but couldn't score. Roscoe's play calling and deceptive fakes
and flips, and the running of Morton and Rankin, led an 84-yard
march to a first-quarter 7–0 lead. Another drive was stopped at
the 3 when a pass intended for Kelley was intercepted in the end
zone, and a third drive was stopped at the 10.

Eleven minutes into the third quarter Fuller was hammered
by halfback Eddie Chamberlain. It felt like he had been hit by
a runaway grand piano. In the huddle he began to argue with
Roscoe about the play being called. "We don't have that play,"
he said.

Curtin called time. Out came Major Wandle. "What's the
score?" he asked Fuller.

"Don't kid me," Fuller said. "I know what the score is."

"Well, what is it?"

Fuller couldn't tell him. He had suffered a concussion and
was done for the day.

The five-foot-six Bob Schultz replaced him. Dartmouth began to roll. One drive made it down to the Yale 11 when Kelley
tore into the backfield and literally threw Rand for a 13-yard loss
on a reverse that Rand momentarily fumbled.

By the fourth quarter the Yale line was wearing down. The
trash talk coming from the green-shirted visitors wasn't bother-
ing them. Grosscup and Kelley were giving it right back. In the
first half they had been mouse-trapping the Dartmouth char-
gers. Now they were getting the same treatment. The sophomore
tackles, Wright and Scott, were being trapped. Denny Myers had
taught them to try to play off the blocker, go into the backfield
about one yard, and stop to see what was happening. Dartmouth
was letting them through then hitting them.

They were being tested relentlessly. At one point, Blaik sent
in an entire fresh team. Pinned deep in their own backyard, Tom
Curtin kicked from his end zone on third down. The kick was

blocked; Meredith Scott pounced on it at the 1. Curtin kicked again. Again it was blocked. This time two Dartmouth men scrambled for it but were unable to contain it until they were out of the end zone for a two-point safety.

After the following punt, Dartmouth's Chamberlain and Handrahan pounded through for three first downs and reached the 13. On one play, guard Webb Davis, only five-foot-seven but full of fight, collided with Chamberlain and was carried off on a stretcher. Charley Strauss replaced Davis, the fourth lineman he had relieved that day. Jack Wright limped off, replaced by Crampton. Even DeAngelis, aching back and all, was pressed into duty for the final three minutes, relieving Grosscup

With an exhausted line playing out of its usual positions, somehow the Bulldogs found the grit to hold on. As the clock ran down with Dartmouth threatening again, three times Kelley, Crampton, and Scott stopped the running backs. On fourth down Scott and Crampton sacked Chamberlain back on the 30, preserving the 7–2 victory.

A minute later the whistle blew, and the exuberant Yale rooters among the forty thousand, unable to tear apart the concrete bowl, poured out of the seats and tore down their own goal posts.

Pond had spent the day plugging holes in the line like a leaking dike. Kelley, Morton, and Train played sixty minutes, Grosscup and Scott fifty-seven each. The *New York Times* called the Yale victory a tribute to "sheer courage and fighting heart" and cited the last quarter as "one of the bravest moments in recent Yale football history."

13 | November 10

THE PRINCETON FOOTBALL SCHEDULE WAS BUILT LIKE THE interstate highway system, with rest stops strategically placed along the way. Lehigh was the next. In Crisler's first year the Tiger had routed the Mountain Hawks, 53–0.

The only thing that had perturbed Crisler in the Harvard game was the number of times the Tiger attack had faltered inside the 20. That was something they had to work on. Otherwise, everybody started looking ahead two weeks to the Yale game. After a light workout on Monday, Crisler gave his starters a day off while the scrubs learned the Lehigh plays to run against the varsity the next two days. On Wednesday he was jolted when Jac Weller limped off the field with a sprained ankle. Weller and Spofford would sit out the Lehigh game. Katz Kadlic would go to New Haven to scout the Yale-Georgia game.

When the score against Lehigh reached 40–0, the third-stringers took over and finished the 54–0 track meet. Thirty-five Tigers saw action. One new play was tried out, a forward pass followed by a lateral to a tackle. Every play involving a lateral had worked so far this season. Despite the lopsided score, Crisler wore a frown when Lehigh staged two goal-line stands, exposing a weakness in Princeton's power plays.

Nobody enjoyed the game more than the Princeton freshmen. That morning the undefeated Tiger frosh team had beaten Yale, 14–0. That victory meant the rule requiring all freshmen to wear black ties would be waived for the day. They came into Palmer Stadium for the Lehigh game carrying their ties knotted in a long banner and draped them over the goal posts at halftime.

Once again undergraduates circulated a petition decrying Princeton's weak schedule. (In 1931, when their only win was against Amherst, the cry was that the schedule was too tough; now the same schedule was said to be too easy.) They called for a post-season charity game against Pittsburgh or Minnesota. But the school's agreement with Yale banning post-season games had been renewed in 1933. Both administrations believed in keeping football in its place.

The Yale coaches were doing some leapfrogging too, looking past the upcoming Georgia game to begin planning for Princeton. They started teaching the scrubs some Princeton plays to run against the varsity.

The week began with a welcome day off for the weary varsity. Kim Whitehead showed up walking without a cane for the first time in a week. He ran laps but took no part in any scrimmages and was a doubtful starter. The line was still unsettled, although it looked like Jimmy DeAngelis might be ready to play on Saturday and Grosscup could go back to guard. Anticipating that Whitehead might not be ready to start, Neale designed a new play for Stan Fuller, a delay where the line would shift to strong side left, the ball would go to Fuller, he would fake handoffs to the other backs while the line let some defenders through, and Fuller would keep the ball and go through the hole at left guard. They practiced it on Tuesday before a heavy rain drove them into Coxe. A rain-slick field on Wednesday limited them to dummy scrimmages until long after the lights were turned on. Greasy Neale ignored the weather. Whether it was practice or a game, he concentrated so intently on what he was watching that he claimed he couldn't tell afterward what the weather had been like.

Before practice on Wednesday a worried Chooch Train walked over to Neale and Pond and said, "I hate to tell y'all how to run your business. I try to keep my mouth shut. But we've been working against Princeton plays and we haven't practiced against

Georgia plays at all. Georgia is coming up here loaded for bear. I just hate to think of us getting beat by them."

Pond said, "We think you're right in a way, but we have got to concentrate on the Princeton game. That's number one. Number two, we've got to take somebody in stride and we think we can do that with Georgia."

Georgia was 3-3 after beating a so-so Florida team, 14–0, the previous Saturday. It had beaten Yale in their last four meetings.

Train said, "Well, I'm from Georgia and I know how those guys are gonna feel when they come up here. They're gonna call every one of us a Yankee so-and-so and they're gonna be out to kick hell out of us."

Thursday they scrimmaged against Georgia plays for two hours. That night Jerry Roscoe ran a fever. The next day he was in the infirmary with the grippe.

Greasy Neale had come to regard Roscoe as the best quarterback in the country and said so publicly. Privately he bolstered Roscoe's confidence by poking his head into Roscoe's room each night. "Who's the greatest quarterback Yale ever had?" he'd ask.

Roscoe would mumble, "Thanks, Greasy."

They would have to rely on Tommy Curtin to call the plays against Georgia.

On this cold overcast Saturday the Yale rooters, huddled under blankets, didn't have much to cheer about.

On Yale's first play after a punt return to the Georgia 47, Tom Curtin called Fuller's new play. It worked to perfection, Fuller raced all the way, and it was suddenly 7–0.

"Then we just quit," Train said. "I never have seen a team just absolutely sit on their butts the way we did."

Georgia's first touchdown came soon after Fuller's when Curtin fumbled on his own 26 and Allen Schi recovered for Georgia. Two plays later Curtin and Rankin missed tackles as Minot ran between them, and it was 7–7.

In the second quarter the Elis reached the Georgia 8, but a pass to Kelley in the end zone was intercepted and they never got that close again.

But Chooch Train didn't know how to quit. On the opening kickoff he had been the first one down the field, dropping the receiver in his tracks at the 15. He was all over the field, chasing down runners in the secondary all afternoon. After the game, Georgia coach Harry Mehre said, "Train was the greatest one-man exhibition I've ever seen in a game."

Chooch had been right about one thing: the Georgia Bull-dogs were mean and nasty and bent on kicking hell out of the Yankee Bulldogs.

Larry Kelley was playing opposite tackle Allen Schi, whom Train had known in Macon, Georgia, as "the dirtiest player any-body ever saw."

By halftime Kelley's face was a bloody mess. "What are they doing to you out there?" Neale asked him.

"Schi has a ring about as big as a rock and every time the ball is snapped he punches me in the face," Kelley said. "He should have been thrown out in the first quarter but they're all pretty bad."

Trying to ease the hostile edge of the Southerners, Train said to one of them, "Hey, you guys know I'm from Georgia?"

They didn't know and they didn't care.

The second half was played almost entirely in Yale terri-tory. Georgia completed only one pass all day but gained twice as much on the ground as Yale. Neale and Pond were using the same seven-man defensive line that had worked against Dart-mouth, but the Georgians were ready for it and exploited it. DeAngelis moved between a tackle and guard, and the speedy Georgia backs tore through the middle. In the third quarter Yale held for three downs inside the 10, but the Georgia line won the battle and scored on the fourth try to take the lead, 14–7.

The fourth quarter was a kicking duel in which neither team could gain an edge, and that's the way it ended.

Maybe the Yale coaches' belief that they could take Georgia "in stride" backfired. They thought they could relax, and it cost them. That may have been the Elis' game in the days of the "smilers," but it was not their game now. It seemed that if they weren't keyed up to fight overwhelming forces, they were flat.

Or maybe it was further evidence of the old adage, "Even your own team is different from one week to the next, and you never know which one will show up."

Or maybe it showed how much they missed Jerry Roscoe. Tom Curtin had completed passes to Kelley, Morton, and Fuller, but he was neither the passer, play caller, nor safety man that Roscoe was.

14 | November 12–16

FRITZ CRISLER WAS NOT HAPPY WITH HIS PLAYERS' PERFOR-
mance against Lehigh, regardless of the score. They had rung up three quick touchdowns on two interceptions and a punt return. All the scoring had been done on long runs. Despite the lopsided score, Lehigh had stopped them twice with goal-line stands. In fact, all of Princeton's scoring all year had come from outside the 10-yard line with one exception.

"This week's preparation for the Yale game will be our hardest series of practices of the year," Crisler said. "It was obvious that our attack needs polishing and we intend to work intensively on fundamentals all week."

Crisler had taken his offensive strength for granted from the start of the season and stressed defense in practice week after week. The day before the Harvard game he had admitted as much to Boston writers. As a result, scouts considered Constable, Kadlic, and LeVan to be even better on defense than offense. Next year, Crisler said, he intended to emphasize offense, introducing new systems used by few other teams.

For the Yale game, he now had Sandbach and John working on quick kicks and kicking field goals from the 25-yard line in case those little-used plays might make the difference.

On Monday he put on his gloomiest face and tried to get them fired up—at him, at themselves, at Yale—by letting them know they had not been much good as a team in the Lehigh game. Then he put them through their hardest practice session of the year. Nobody was excused.

Both teams had been scouting each other all season. The weekly reports on Yale reflected a team that had made steady progress. Katz Kadlic had skipped the Lehigh game to watch the Bulldogs play Georgia. It didn't matter to Crisler how late he might learn something that he could use. (Last year in Providence to play Brown, some of his players had slipped out of the hotel for some fun and run into some gabby Brown players on the same mission. They learned that Brown planned to surprise them with a five-man line on defense. The Princeton players woke Crisler in the middle of the night and told him. Saturday morning Crisler got his team up early and took them to the hotel ballroom, where he worked out plays to use against such an alignment. They had little trouble beating Brown, 33–0. Crisler had waited until Monday to punish his midnight scouts.)

The ground attack was sound. Crisler's new plays for the week expanded the passing game, especially long passes, which would be a departure from Princeton's usual pattern, something Yale scouts hadn't seen.

The third team was drilled in copying Yale's spinners, reverses, fake kick formations, passes, and laterals and ran them against the first and second teams on Wednesday. Thursday the varsity worked on new plays against the gray-shirt scrubs.

Crisler knew that Greasy Neale preferred to kick off to start a game. That suited Crisler; he preferred to receive. The Tigers had scored several touchdowns on the opening kickoff by massing their blocking on the right side and leading the runner up the sideline. This time they would fool Yale by putting the blocking on the left and going up the left side. "The adrenaline is always flowing furiously at the start of any Yale-Princeton game," said Gil Lea. "The plan was to score on the kickoff, throw them off balance, get the momentum going, and run up the score before the Bulldogs knew what hit them."

Whoever won the toss, that's the way the game would start. That was the plan, anyhow.

For the first time all year, Princeton was at full strength. Everybody was ready to play. Spofford, who had been out since dislocating his shoulder in the Amherst game, and guard Jack Irwin, out since a pre-season knee injury, were declared fit.

Betting was light in Princeton. Regardless of the New York odds, which heavily favored Princeton, 5 to 3 was the best a local Yale rooter could find.

Before Friday's practice Crisler said, "Previous scores and previous showings mean nothing when this game comes around. This is a good Yale team and it's going to play its best football tomorrow. We've scouted them and we know what we're talking about. I believe and hope we're ready for a real game of football for there certainly is one coming up."

If there was any overconfidence among his highly talented players, Crisler was doing his best to deflate it. They had been the undefeated idols, the gods, the darlings of the students and alumni for two years. Writers from Grantland Rice through the ranks of New York and national columnists had written glowingly about them. But where was the line between confidence and overconfidence?

Early arrivals from New Haven were already parading through the town, painting a blue "Y" on everything in sight. After a light workout and dinner, Crisler put his players on buses and took them six miles away to Lawrenceville Prep for the night to get away from the noise and distractions of the start of the biggest social weekend of the year.

Bob Hall was a Philadelphia lawyer who had been a 135-pound quarterback and blocking back for Yale in 1927–29, then coached at Roxbury while going to law school. In September Malcolm Farmer had asked him to go to every Princeton game and make notes, then prepare a scouting report for Ducky Pond and Greasy Neale. He could enlist as many assistants as he wanted. They would be paid a small fee plus expenses. (Athletic department books show a total expenditure of $1,793 for scouting. Odd entries show Hall receiving $100 on November 12, Robert Ward $50 on October 29, and C. S. Osborne $15 per game.)

Other schools, like Harvard, might have two men scouting Princeton and two following Yale. Hall called on other Yale men, including his former roommate, Robert Bandeer, and friends who had played at other eastern schools, to join him. Each week they numbered at least six pairs of experienced eyes—sometimes as many as nine—watching every move of every Tiger. Each man took one or two positions to watch on offense and defense and noted whatever their man did on each play. After the game they got together and went through the entire game play by play, position by position. Then they pooled their observations on attitudes, play patterns, strengths, and weaknesses. They tried to predict what plays Princeton might use in certain situations the following week.

"We were aware of every type of play they might run," Hall said.

Hall knew some of the players from his prep school coaching days. The Kaufman brothers had played for him. Les Kaufman was fast as a streak, but Hall knew he could be discouraged if he was hit hard and often. Princeton called defensive signals for the entire defense working as a unit. On punts the guards were the first down field, not the ends. Princeton backs were as good defensively as on offense, maybe better. All that went into the reports.

On Saturday night after the Princeton-Lehigh game, Hall worked late putting together six weeks' worth of scouting notes. That night and all day Sunday his wife worked at the typewriter. On Monday morning the seventy-six-page, single-spaced report was handed to Ducky Pond.

Hall's strongest warning: "Garry LeVan's open-field running is Princeton's most dangerous offensive weapon. Never let him get his hands on a kickoff or a punt."

Greasy Neale read that and walked over to Stan Fuller. "Fuller," Neale said, "we're going to have you kick out of bounds whenever possible on Saturday. We've got to keep the ball away from Garry LeVan. He's dynamite."

Neale put a red flag at each end of the goal line of the practice field and two more at the 20-yard line. He said to Fuller, "I want you to practice all week kicking out of bounds between those flags. And if you kick one to LeVan Saturday I'll take you out of the game."

Early in the year the coaches had invited LeRoy Mills, a Princeton star of thirty years earlier and a kicking tutor, to come to Yale and give the kickers some pointers. Now those sessions came back to Fuller:

"The first thing Mills had done was blindfold us and tell us to go through the steps of punting. If you kicked it out of bounds it meant you were off balance. If you kicked it straight you were okay. Since you kick it with the side of your foot, if you face straight ahead and try to kick it out of bounds on the right, it's dangerous. If you don't quite hit it right, you might shank it and boot it maybe ten yards before it goes out. You're always trying to kick it straight. So I had to turn my body and try to kick them out on the left side. That way if I sliced it too much it would at least go straight downfield."

Fuller made up his mind he wasn't going to aim for the 20. He wanted to nail them inside the 5. Mills told him that was too ambitious; too many would go over the goal line and he'd be giving them 20 yards. "Don't give them anything," Mills preached. But Fuller was going to do it his way.

Of course, when he was deep in his own territory, he had to kick for distance. He practiced kicking line drives, not high, arcing "pretty" punts, aiming for yardage-eating bounces.

He also worked at getting a kick away in under two seconds from the time it left the center's hands. Hoping to shave a half-second and lessen the chance of its being blocked, he stepped back with his left foot, then started forward with it just as he got the ball, putting his full body behind the kick.

Monday afternoon practice at Yale was devoted to a blackboard session. The coaches discussed their concerns about the weakness in the center of the line in the Georgia game. On Tuesday they went through a light workout. Jerry Roscoe was out of the infirmary but not in uniform. There would be no scrimmaging this week, just signal drilling, working on timing and precision, and taking a look at Princeton plays run by the scrubs. Yale didn't use defensive signals; each man knew his assignment. There was some improvising. Train and Scott might decide between them who would do what just before a play. If the play didn't come at Train, Train went after the play, wherever it ran. Kelley was something of a free-lancer. If he sniffed out a play, he might leave his position and chase it, sometimes to glorious, sometimes to ignominious, effect. DeAngelis and Whitehead were the linebackers, moving with the play. When they nabbed a ball carrier, they did it in tandem. One would hit him high and the other low, the high tackler aiming to jar loose the ball.

Greasy Neale liked to say he could always cook up one play to win a game. Driven indoors by rain and wind and snow flurries on Thursday, he stood before a blackboard and announced, "Here is the play that can win the Princeton game." All season the number 21 pass pattern had been Kelley down and out from right end, Morton out of the backfield down and in, and Train from left end down and out. Roscoe had the option to throw to any one of them. He threw to Morton more often than the others. They were sure the Princeton scouts had noted it. They also expected the Princeton secondary to focus on Kelley. On Saturday, Neale explained, they would switch; Morton would go down and out, Kelley would cut across the middle. The idea was to cause some confusion among the Princeton secondary. Neale added a twist: they would run it from a fake punt formation to freeze the Princeton backs. Fuller would line up behind center with Roscoe to his right. The ball would go to Roscoe, who would take a few steps behind Fuller while Fuller went through the motions of punting.

All during this week of preparation most pundits were skeptical of Yale's chances. A typical approach was the one by Fred Grimsley in the *Hartford Times*: "Still hoping to hold the Princeton score to a minimum this weekend, while at the same time hoping that his own offensive will click sufficiently to overcome the Tiger's certain tallies, Head Coach Ducky Pond worked his men diligently yesterday on the defensive."

While most carefree limb-perchers called Princeton a shoo-in, a three- touchdown favorite, wiser heads tiptoed around guessing the outcome of this tradition-soaked battle.

The *Daily Princetonian* cautioned, "So many times have Yale and Princeton teams upset predictions, the wise prophet has ceased to predict anything but a bitterly fought contest."

Still, football writers were paid to be prophets, so prophesy they did:

Damon Runyon had no doubts at all about the outcome. "Princeton plays Yale at Princeton, but this is a pop-over for Princeton. The best those who journey to see it will get is a case of chilblains. Princeton can play team No. 3 against Yale today and win."

"If both teams play according to form, Princeton should win by three touchdowns and up" (unsigned *Time Out* column).

"On strict playing form, I should say that Princeton is at least three touchdowns better than Yale. Yale's unusually strong endplay should be a factor in her defensive strength. If there is any weakness in Princeton I should say it is too much material to be coordinated into one unit. Yale has only an outside chance to win" (Grantland Rice).

"You ask for a lengthy forecast on tomorrow's game. Unfortunately, I can think of only one word in connection with this game and it is: Princeton" (Bill Corum, *New York Journal*).

"Why drag an innocent bystander into the pit, when the bulldog is due for the annual whirlwind debate with the tiger. But there is no escape short of fleeing the country. The opinion is this: the undefeated Princeton team is stronger than the lineup of Yale. All the Princetons have to do is prove it" (John Kieran, *New York Times*).

Nobody out-and-out picked Yale to win, but there were hedgers:

"I do look for this Yale team to conduct itself gallantly and perhaps surprisingly" (Charles E. Parker, *New York World-Telegram*).

"Yale has a fighting chance to beat Princeton. This conviction is based on seeing Yale against Columbia, Army, and Dartmouth in turn and by recognizing a sure development, steady improvement under a sound coaching policy, and the high spirit of the players. . . . Princeton should win, but there is something more in this game of football than manpower and the high skill of individuals. This something more is largely psychological and is of the spirit" (George Daley, *New York Herald Tribune*).

The Princeton beat writer for the *Trenton Evening Times* wrote, "Yale hopes to get the jump. So does Princeton. The jump counts for a lot in these great traditional games. Stage fright in the opening quarter has in previous years often had a serious effect on the outcome of the game, as the psychological advantage of scoring in the opening moments of the contest has endowed the team drawing first blood with a driving spirit which the efforts of superior ability has been unable to overcome."

Fritz Crisler and Greasy Neale differed on how to get that jump. Neale wanted the burden of early jitters on the other team deep in its own backyard, where mistakes might be costly. Crisler believed his juggernaut was capable of striking quickly and setting the other side back on its heels, where it might not recover. They both knew that whoever won the toss, Yale would kick off.

They also both knew that none of this was necessarily so. Last year Yale had scored first on a safety after blocking a kick but wound up being crushed, 27–2.

All of which went to prove, wrote the Trenton sage, that "anything can happen in a Princeton-Yale football encounter, and . . . the estimations of the most expert grid authorities of the land will most probably count for naught when the actual returns of the game are turned in."

If anyone believed in omens, the Yale jayvees handed the

Princeton jayvees their first loss, 6–0, on University Field on Friday afternoon.

Thursday evening Pat Garvan had a hunch. He liked what he had seen of the team's practice that week. He felt the spirit of determination that went into it and the sense of confidence that filled the field house. He walked a few blocks from campus and found a bookie who offered him 5-to-1 odds and bet $1,000 on Yale to beat Princeton. He could afford it.

Lou Walker, one of the assistant managers, also had a feeling that the Bulldogs would be up for this game. But he didn't have any money. He had a friend who was a regular customer of a bookie named Morris Elman. Walker telephoned Elman, took a deep breath, and said, "Morris, I'd like to bet $500 on Yale. You ought to give me about 20 points."

"I don't give points," Elman said, "But I'll give you 5-to-1 odds."

"I don't have the money," Walker said. "Will you take it on credit?"

Elman agreed.

If he lost, Walker knew his father, wealthy St. Louis investment banker George H. Walker, would kill him for gambling on a football game. If he had to, he'd go to his sister's husband, Prescott S. Bush, a Yale man now on Wall Street, for a loan.

At 10 a.m. Friday twenty-nine members of the football squad; four student managers; coaches Pond, Neale, Williamson, Scott, and Myers—all but Myers accompanied by their wives; Major Wandle; team physician Dr. Seabury; and a few dozen favored other men not part of the team boarded two reserved Pullman cars on the Number 7 train leaving New Haven for the three hour and twenty minute ride to Princeton. They had lunch on the train, every man signing his own check.

"Forget that Georgia game," an unnamed Yale rooter who

had accompanied the team told reporters who met the train on its arrival at Princeton Station. "This bunch has been going great guns this week and if they continue there's a very fine chance of a grand upset tomorrow. They may have too many for us, but our first string is certainly ready and primed for action. You may see some fireworks tomorrow."

Buses took the players to McCormick Field House, where they dressed for a light workout at Palmer Stadium from 2 to 3:30: limbering-up exercises, a little passing, a refresher on Princeton plays, nothing strenuous. But they seemed out of sync. "I guess we were nervous," said Bob Train. "We looked horrible." Then they boarded buses to the Hotel Stacy-Trent, twelve miles away in Trenton, where they would stay the night. The printed itinerary given to each man called for dinner in the varsity private dining room at 6:00 p.m., and at 6:45 "Varsity goes to movies." Lights out was at 10 p.m. The players were all on the fifth floor; twelve had roommates: Larry Kelley and Jack Wright, Bernie Rankin and Johnny Hersey, Clare Curtin and Joe Johnson, Ben Grosscup and Ed King, Strat Morton and John Overall, Bob Schultz and Bob Train. The rest had single rooms. Beside each player's bed was a half-gallon bottle of Chippewa spring water— the itinerary warned "DRINK ONLY SPECIAL WATER AT ALL TIMES"— and a big red apple.

15 | November 17, Pre-Game

THE WAKE-UP CALLS AT THE STACY-TRENT HOTEL CAME AT 8:00. Breakfast at 8:30 was followed by a board talk. Then everybody reported to Major Wandle in room 505 to have their ankles taped. They ate lunch at 11:00; the buses to McCormick Field House left at noon.

The bus ride was eerily quiet. Nobody spoke. Outwardly they

were calm, but an intense inner nervous excitement they had never known—the tension felt by every challenger or champion before a big event—coursed through their veins and into their brains. Each man was deep in his own thoughts.

Larry Kelley was nervous and sweating. He felt weak. His stomach was churning. But he was like that every Saturday morning before a game, so he was used to it. He knew that once the kickoff occurred, it would all go away. He thought about his high school coach back in Williamsport, Pennsylvania. Kelley had played only one year, his senior year, and hadn't been very good. When his coach had heard that Kelley was going to Yale, he said, "Larry will have to pay his way in to the games."

"On the basis of my one year's play for him, he was right," Kelley thought. He had gone to Peddie Prep, in Princeton's backyard. There his coach, a Yale alum named Earl MacArthur, had worked with him and told him he would make the grade at Yale. And here he was, the starting end in his sophomore year. He didn't feel like he was part of any team of destiny or anything like that and didn't think anybody else felt that way. They knew they were underdogs and were just determined to do their best.

Clare Curtin had been pointing to this day ever since the Tiger had beaten them last year. He was fed up with reading all that stuff about how the great Fritz Crisler had come from Minnesota to Princeton to lead the team into destiny. He'd never felt this kind of personal antagonism against any other team. Some of the others he'd talked to felt the same way. He had sensed a different atmosphere about the team during the preceding week. If each man was determined to succeed and they worked together, they could hold their own and knock them off.

Chooch Train didn't go for all that talk about "something different in the air" during the week's practice. All he knew was that Princeton had a hell of a team. "If we can get in there and slug away we can give them a good scare," he thought.

Jerry Roscoe didn't need any gung-ho talk either. He knew they were all pretty psyched up already. He went over the game plan Greasy Neale had designed for him. He had complete confidence in Neale, whom he considered the strength of the coaching staff. Princeton was such a high-scoring team, while Yale had scored more than two touchdowns only once, against Brown. They would have to play a defensive game.

It seemed to Stan Fuller as if half his life passed through his mind during that one-hour bus ride. Nobody had traveled so far or overcome so many obstacles to be there. In high school in Erie everything had been athletics. He was the star runner, blocker, and kicker. He was not college material and he knew it. But he received scholarship offers from Big Ten schools who offered to send him to Lake Forest Prep School for a year. He was all set to go when a teammate who was then at Roxbury Prep wrote to him urging him to go there, even lined up sponsors in Erie to pay his way. It was one of those moments, Fuller mused, like they talk about that change a man's life. The Roxbury coaches, including Bob Hall, were all Yale men. They pushed him to go to Yale. But after two and a half years at Roxbury, Yale rejected him. It looked like he'd never get there. A friend suggested he apply to Princeton; they turned him down too. If they hadn't, he might have been in Lawrenceville last night. He refused to give up. Bob Hall encouraged him to go to a school in Ohio, work to meet the requirements, not play football, then transfer.

In the summer of 1932 Fuller had finally made it into Yale, but he had to sit out a year as a transfer student. In '33 he was hampered by a charley horse that turned into a bone growth that sidelined him much of the year.

Now, five and a half years after he had left Erie, he was a senior, playing his next to last game for Yale. The newspapers all week had listed Bernie Rankin as starting halfback, with no mention of Fuller. But he knew better. He didn't care for Greasy

Neale, but he had done the job for Neale, primarily as a blocker and punter, playing in every game. Neale had told him he would be doing the punting today.

The stardom promised by his high school days had eluded him. As he looked out the window and saw the Princeton tower come into view, he said to himself, "This is my one day. This is my chance."

An hour before the kickoff the Bulldogs changed at McCormick Field House and walked the quarter mile across the practice field and into the open end of the concrete horseshoe. They jogged a lap or two around the track that circled the field, stretching their legs, loosening up, tossing the ball around, some snapping drills with a sub quarterback calling signals to get the line working in unison.

Meredith Scott was crouching, his head near the turf, when he looked up and saw an orange-and-black-clad figure come through the open end across the field, followed by another and another; the line kept getting longer and longer until it stretched the entire hundred yards along the sideline.

Scott was stunned. "They were silhouetted against the sky and looked pretty dadgum imposing," he said.

The others saw it too. It looked to them as if Fritz Crisler had suited up the varsity, the jayvees, the 115-pounders, the freshmen, and even, Stan Fuller thought, "some people who never played football. It looked like we were going to be subbed against all day."

Clare Curtin thought, "Another one of Fritz Crisler's psychological tricks."

Greasy Neale saw the looks of consternation on the faces of his younger players. He said, "Don't pay any attention to 'em. They still have to take down their britches to shit."

Everybody laughed. It broke the tension.

The twenty-nine Yale men and their coaches went up a ramp in the closed end and around to a small pre-game and halftime meeting room under the stands where they ran into another of Crisler's tricks. There was a wood-burning potbellied stove in the room. The last time they had been there, in 1932—Crisler's first year—it was a cold day and the stove was cold, and they had complained about it. Today it was warm; the stove was fired up and red hot; the windows were nailed shut, and it was suffocating in the tiny room. Ducky Pond went into a frenzy trying to put out the fire and break open the windows, all the time ranting about Crisler's trying to intimidate them. They had never seen him so worked up over anything.

Pond then called out the names of the starters: linemen Train, Scott, Clare Curtin, DeAngelis, Grosscup, Wright, Kelley; backs Roscoe, Fuller, Morton, Whitehead. Some of them were surprised when he said "Fuller" and not "Rankin." (The program showed Rankin starting. After the game started, the radio announcer, Ted Husing, kept calling Fuller "Rankin" until someone corrected him.)

It was the first time these eleven had ever started together.

The subs then left the room.

Ducky Pond had calmed down to his usual low-key demeanor. "We've done our best to prepare you. You know what to anticipate."

"I was willing to be swept into a fervor with a coach's pep talk," Clare Curtin said, "but we didn't need it that day. It wasn't a gung-ho thing. It was an inner feeling."

On the other side of the field, Fritz Crisler was firing psychological weapons of a different kind. The Princeton winning streak meant a lot to him. "It was the only game where you could sense a certain tenseness in Crisler," said Gil Lea.

"Gentlemen," he said, "this is the most important game of the year. Princeton alumni all over the world have their eyes on you. We can beat them, but they've come down here to play ball."

He read off the starters: linemen Delaney, Stoess, Bliss, Kalbaugh, John, Chamberlain, Lea; backs Kadlic, Sandbach, LeVan, Constable.

Then, Ben Delaney later recalled, Crisler said, "Gentlemen, this is the last game for the seniors against Yale. I think it would be good if we coaches got out of here and left the meeting to the seniors."

The coaches walked out.

The seniors—Constable, Kadlic, Kalbaugh, Delaney—looked at each other. Delaney spoke up. "This is my last Yale game. It's Katz's last one, Pepper's last one, Mose's last one. We have a chance to be national champs two years in a row. There's a lot of tradition here and we're part of it."

The younger players were all fired up.

Delaney said, "It was very emotional. We came out of there practically in tears. I think it backfired. It would have been better if Fritz had acted like we were playing Brown or Amherst."

They lined up on the sidelines for the national anthem, twenty-nine blue-shirted Yale Bulldogs opposite a hundred or more in orange and black.

The program listed forty-five men—four full teams—for Princeton, thirty for Yale.

The Yale line narrowly outweighed the Tiger line on average, 183 to 178 pounds. Only Clare Curtin topped 200 for Yale. Both backfields averaged 166, but that figure was misleading. The fullbacks, Whitehead and Constable, weighed about 180 each; the quarterbacks, Roscoe and Kadlic, weighed about 156 each. Garry LeVan was even smaller.

The captains, Curtin and Kalbaugh, met in midfield. Curtin called heads and won the toss and elected to kick.

Then the Yale starters huddled, hands grasped. "Let's go get 'em," said Clare Curtin.

16 | November 17, First Quarter

JERRY ROSCOE TILTED THE BALL ON THE GROUND (THEY USED no tees), and Clare Curtin booted it. Determined to keep it away from Garry LeVan, he aimed for the corner, but it went out of bounds. He had to kick again. Everybody's wound-up nerves remained tight a little longer. This time he lofted one high and long. When Clare Curtin got a good long kick away, he liked to stand and watch it fly, like a modern home run hitter before he goes into his trot around the bases. Curtin was in no hurry to race downfield to be in on the tackle. Everybody else was. The adrenaline erupted, and everything they had been taught about the new touchback rules at the start of the season flew out of their heads. (Downing the ball or tackling the receiver in the end zone brought the ball out to the 20.)

Ken Sandbach caught the ball, then dropped it at the 1, and it rolled into the end zone as the Princeton cordon of interference formed to his left and a thundering herd of blue shirts bore down on his right with only one thing in their minds: get him, wherever he was. Sandbach thought only of getting out to where his blockers were massed waiting to escort him unmolested down the sideline.

Kelley and Scott and Train and DeAngelis were trying to chase him down in the end zone; Sandbach was trying to get out of the end zone instead of just going to the ground.

"We were two teams that didn't know what they were doing," Kelley said. "We were all wrong."

Sandbach scrambled out a few feet over the line, where Train and DeAngelis brought him down.

"The letdown was palpable," said Princeton end Gil Lea. "We were all set up, the blocking in place to go down and score and here we were on our 1-yard line. If we had scored on that kickoff we would have whipped them badly."

The Tigers were dazed. They had never started a game from that position. There was nothing in Katz Kadlic's experience or playbook to deal with it. He could not look to or even at the scowling Fritz Crisler for help. Kadlic elected to get out of the hole by punting on first down.

LeVan's kick was caught by Roscoe on the 40 and run back 10 yards.

The Elis were geared up to a level they'd never experienced. They felt the tailwind of momentum behind them. Then something else hit them.

On the first play, center Jimmy DeAngelis discerned what he believed to be another part of Fritz Crisler's game plan: intimidation and mayhem. Crisler knew how thin Yale's material was; the more starters knocked out of action, the weaker they'd become. DeAngelis went up to the line and saw guard Jac Weller facing him. Weller outweighed him by fifty pounds. Just before the snap, Weller charged and knocked him five yards through the air.

"Maybe he was just steamed up," DeAngelis said, "but I don't believe it."

The offside penalty brought the ball to the 25.

There was no maybe about Yale's being steamed up. The Bulldogs were offside twice in the next three plays, a series that ended when Roscoe threw a pass in the flats that Mose Kalbaugh intercepted on the 28 and returned to the Yale 48. Greasy Neale winced: bad play call.

Fumbles were to Fritz Crisler what bases on balls were to baseball managers—life shorteners. On Pepper Constable's second plunge into the line, Ben Grosscup hit him so hard that the ball popped out and Kim Whitehead was there to recover it on the 44. The coach's frown deepened.

Two plays netted a few yards. On third down Stan Fuller got

off his first punt of the day. It eluded Garry LeVan but failed to find the sidelines and rolled into the end zone.

After yielding a first down on the ground, the Yale line held firm on the Princeton 34. It was about this time that Ben Grosscup noticed that the Princeton center, Mose Kalbaugh, dragged the ball an inch or two along the ground before he snapped it. Grosscup had played enough center to know that the officials would place it the way the center wanted it and there was no turning or shifting it after that. The defense could start as soon as the ball was moved in any way. During a time-out Grosscup told his line, "Back up a little off the line and when he starts inching it you take off." They timed their charge by Kalbaugh's motion, and on the snap they were going full bore.

"We were in their backfield all day," Grosscup said.

That's why when LeVan went back to punt this time, a quartet of blue jerseys swarmed into the backfield. One man got a hand on the ball, and it wobbled out of bounds on the Yale 46.

On a shovel pass, Whitehead went around right end for 6, then plowed into the line for 3 more but was stopped cold on third down. Fuller kicked and missed the coffin corner, and the ball went into the end zone.

Starting again at the 20, LeVan fumbled the first snap from center but saved Fritz Crisler more anguish by falling on it for a 4-yard loss. Sandbach tried the line and got nowhere. The Tiger was clearly discombobulated. His timing was off. The blocking wasn't moving anybody. Every time the Bulldogs stopped a runner, their confidence grew. They were using a 6-2-2-1 defense, with Grosscup and Whitehead the linebackers, Fuller and Morton the secondary, and Roscoe the safety. Grosscup followed the flow of every play and was demonic in his determination to thwart it. All afternoon he would torment his counterpart, guard Frank John, taking him out like a teardrop wiped up by a tissue. When either of the young sophomore tackles, Wright or Scott, missed a tackle or an assignment, Grosscup was there with an encouraging word.

LeVan backed up a little farther and kicked on third down. Morton caught it at the Princeton 42 and was quickly knocked out of bounds. Morton gained 2, tried it again, and was thrown for a 5-yard loss by Gil Lea.

Both quarterbacks had been calling a conservative game, tending to give the ball to the same carrier for two or three plays in a row. Princeton had yet to throw a pass, but then, it had been out of the shadow of its own goal posts only once, for two plays. Jerry Roscoe had stuck to the ground since being intercepted by Kalbaugh.

Roscoe now decided it was time to call number 21, Greasy Neale's special game-winner of the week. Fuller lined up to take the snap, Roscoe on his right and a few steps in front of him. LeVan backed up to receive the kick. The snap went to Roscoe. Fuller faked a kicking motion as Roscoe circled behind him past midfield. The Princeton backs froze, unable to see that Roscoe had the ball. The Yale tackles brush-blocked their men and headed downfield as if in pursuit of the receiver. Morton went around right end past Kelley into the flats. Kelley went down about ten yards and cut toward the middle inside the 30. Train went straight ahead from left end as a potential blocker if the pass went to Kelley. Grosscup pulled back and joined Fuller to protect Roscoe on the right. Whitehead was blocking on the left.

Princeton right end Gil Lea saw Roscoe fade back with the ball, got away from Whitehead, raced for Roscoe, thinking, "Gotcha," and hit him chest high just as Roscoe let the ball go.

"I thought I had him flat on his rear end before he could throw it," Lea said. "How he got it off I'll never know."

Morton was all alone on the right, with about ten yards between him and Sandbach in front of him and Mose Kalbaugh racing to cover him. Kelley was running across the field around the 22. Constable was on his left between him and the line of scrimmage. LeVan and Kadlic had come up on his right to about the 15. Chooch Train was in front of him. The pass headed for Kelley was high, intentionally high. In practice Roscoe had always thrown high to Kelley, who was taller than most backs, and had the agility, reach, and big hands of the first baseman that he was. Kelley was surprised; he didn't expect it. He would always maintain that Roscoe just threw it over the middle, where Morton usually was, by habit. Roscoe was equally adamant that Kelley was his target from the start, coverage or no coverage. Kim Whitehead was surprised. Grosscup and DeAngelis weren't. To them, Kelley was the go-to man, the one who always seemed to make things happen.

"I don't care if there were five men around Kelley," DeAngelis said. "I would throw to him."

LeVan and Kadlic expected the high throw to go over Kelley's head and set their hands ready to intercept it. Kelley went up in the air, fingertipped it with his big right hand, juggled it for about two strides, and tucked it under his left arm.

Extraordinary athletes possess instincts and the ability to process bits of data under pressure at seemingly superhuman speeds. As Kelley came down with the ball, there flashed in his mind the words of football great Red Grange: "When you snag a pass, the natural thing is to plow straight ahead."

Had he headed straight for the goal line, LeVan and Kadlic would have nailed him. He continued toward the sidelines. Train threw himself at Kadlic and LeVan and knocked them off stride long enough to allow Kelley to turn the corner and head down the sideline for the goal line. (Train's action may have saved the play, but fifty years later he was still upset by the *New York Times* photo taken just after he had thrown the key block and fallen to the ground. "It makes me look like a boob," he lamented. "I fell down and there I am on my butt and my hands up in the air in the photo.")

Kadlic and LeVan had regained their balance and were coming after Kelley. Sandbach was also headed for the corner. Kelley eluded Kadlic at about the 10-yard line. LeVan and Sandbach raced to knock him out of bounds at the 5. Just then another image popped up in Kelley's mind.

"As I neared the goal line, the time in the Army game when I had followed Greasy Neale's 'dive for it' and I dove and nearly got my back broken flashed through my head," Kelley said. "Now I'm going up the sideline about the same distance from the goal line and I see these two guys [LeVan and Sandbach] coming toward me and I said to myself, 'No way I'm going to do that again.' So I just stopped and they slid by me and I walked in."

There was no emotional celebration, no high-fives. That wasn't part of the game in those days. Besides, this game was far from over. They still had a big job ahead of them.

Clare Curtin kicked the extra point. Yale led, 7–0.

(According to Jac Weller, Fritz Crisler was sure he had seen Kelley bumped out of bounds when the play had started near the right hash mark—on the Princeton side of the field—making him an ineligible receiver. "He chewed on it all weekend after the game," Weller said, "but decided not to say anything about it. Many times in the future, after a few beers, he would claim he saw Kelley step out of bounds.")

On Curtin's kickoff, caught by Sandbach at the 2 and run back to the 27, there was another attempt to dispatch one of the Yale starters. This one almost succeeded.

Kim Whitehead was clipped on the runback, but no clipping penalty was called. "I had my eyes on the runner and a Princeton guy hit me from the side, a real croaker," Whitehead said. He didn't get up.

His damaged right knee, which had kept him out of the

Dartmouth game and limited his time in the Georgia game, had taken the brunt of the blow. Roscoe called time, and Major Wandle came out with his cart.

"This knee has had it," Whitehead said. "I don't think I can operate on it. Better get somebody up to take my place."

"Let me look at it," Wandle said.

He gave Whitehead a shot of painkiller. "Get up and try it a little longer and see what happens," the major said.

Whitehead tried it a little longer and a little longer—until the game was over.

On Princeton's second play after the kickoff return, LeVan fumbled for the third time; Fuller recovered it on the 34, and Mr. Gloom's mood grew darker.

After three plays made no headway, Fuller punted for the coffin corner but missed again, and the ball rolled into the end zone. At least he had kept it away from Garry LeVan.

The quarter ended with Princeton on its 22, third and 8.

17 | November 17, Second Quarter

THE SECOND QUARTER BEGAN AS A KICKING CONTEST BETWEEN Hugh MacMillan, who had replaced Ben Delaney at left end, and Stan Fuller, interrupted when MacMillan intercepted a Roscoe pass in the flats at the Elis' 47—the same mistake that had produced the same result in the first quarter. Greasy Neale made a mental note to include *that* on next summer's quarterback questionnaire.

If Fritz Crisler ever suffered from an ulcer in the years to come, it may have been born around 2:30 on this beautiful afternoon in Palmer Stadium. After Constable plowed through the line for 5 yards, Homer Spofford, who had replaced Sandbach at left halfback, came around on a reverse and fumbled—the Tigers' fourth of the day—and Jack Wright fell on it at the 41.

This may have been when the bantering began.

Larry Kelley already had a reputation as a wisecracker, one that would grow in the next two years, enhanced by the press with as many invented as genuine Kelleyisms. Despite his later protestations that "when your stomach is churning and your armpits are sweating and you're weak as a kitten, you didn't think of much to say," his teammates were quick to confirm, "Kelley was always talking across the line no matter who we were playing, so there's no reason to think he was quiet this time."

Ben Grosscup was another chatterer.

Some of the cracks dealt with Princeton officials having turned down the Rose Bowl bid last year, as in: "Send us a postcard from the Rose Bowl." After the latest fumble, one of them—Kelley said it wasn't him; Grosscup admitted he might have been the one—said, "Hey, does the Rose Bowl have handles on it?"

When the other side rode Kelley, he hollered back, "I didn't know you guys speak English."

Katz Kadlic seemed befuddled at times when plays didn't work, and Grosscup got on him: "Send Constable through center" and "Show us what you did against Amherst."

As their confidence grew, even the quiet sophomore Meredith Scott got caught up in it. "I did a fair amount of talking," he said, "like when they were starting to call a play, I'd holler, 'We're going to stay in your backfield all afternoon.'"

Sure, some of the remarks were sophomoric, but Kelley and Scott were, after all, sophomores, keyed up to a height of spirits they'd never experienced. Most of the Elis knew some Princeton players from their days as teammates or opponents in prep schools. There was no rancor or animosity in it.

Chooch Train was not usually a talker. "I learned in prep school to keep my mouth shut, cause I knew if I said something,

I would hear, 'Okay, you son of a bitch, I'm gonna get you,' and then they'd get me."

But Train did say something that day. On running plays the Princeton wingback, Les Kaufman, was supposed to block Train. But Kaufman kept missing his block, and the fullback, Pepper Constable, had to take Train out. He did it by grabbing Train's leg and holding him. Chooch had played against Constable for six years beginning in prep school, and they had become friends, so he felt comfortable telling him, "Hey, you're holding me. You can't do that."

"I know it," Constable said. "That's the only way I can stop you. Go over and tell the ref if you want to."

Train did. The ref said, "I didn't see it."

But the Bulldog didn't lose sight of the unfinished business at hand.

Having recovered the fumble, Yale fell short of a first down. This time Fuller landed one out of bounds at the Princeton 27. The Tiger attack still seemed at sixes and sevens. One of Crisler's new pass plays failed again. A tricky reverse went awry.

Then the time bomb exploded.

Led by pulling guard Bill Montgomery, Garry LeVan started toward Train then cut back inside tackle, inside the linebackers Whitehead and DeAngelis, who were heading toward the play, behind Montgomery's block on Roscoe, and headed down the sideline toward the same corner where Kelley had scored.

Train's prep school coach had branded in his brain, "Never give up on a play or quit chasing it." That had kicked into action as soon as he saw LeVan make the first cut away from him. He turned and ran across the field at an angle, and by the time LeVan broke into the open, Train was even with him. He put on a burst of speed and collided with LeVan, knocking him out of bounds at the Yale 25.

Kadlic, having his worst game of the year, slipped trying

to make a shovel pass but held onto the ball for a loss. He then called for some razzle-dazzle, a three-way lateral, LeVan to Mac-Millan to Spofford, who went around right end. Princeton had been sending a pair of blockers at Train on such plays. Rather than try to deal with this tandem, Train would give up a yard or two and make the tackle a few yards downfield. They gained about 3 yards on what Train later called the worst play he had made all year. On third down LeVan passed to MacMillan, who got away from the secondary and reached the 4-yard line before Roscoe could stop him.

The Princeton crowd had its first opportunity to howl. The concrete bowl came as close to rocking as it ever would. On the Yale bench assistant manager Lou Walker was fretting about his bet.

But the Bulldogs on the field were unperturbed. Larry Kelley said, "We didn't even know the crowd was there. Your mind and concentration was all on the game."

Ben Grosscup agreed. "We were so worked up we didn't hear anything or think anything but what we were doing. We were confident, not intimidated."

In one of several inexplicable series of plays called by Kadlic that day, Kadlic sent LeVan instead of his pile-driving fullback Pepper Constable into the line on first down. Kelley tossed him down a half yard beyond the line. On second down Kadlic handed off to Spofford, who tried to push through Scott and Curtin but gained only about a yard. Now Kadlic turned to Constable, who banged into a wall named Curtin, DeAngelis, and Grosscup. A relieved Chooch Train was thankful they had not tried his side again. If they had and he had made the play the same way as the last one, they would have scored.

Fourth and goal. Kadlic reached into the grab bag and pulled out one of Fritz Crisler's new plays, left 33. Gil Lea explained: "It was a trap block play. The right halfback goes out about three yards and then cuts directly in. The trap is to get the Yale tackle

[Wright] to come in, then block him and leave an opening in the line. Homer Spofford was the carrier. It worked perfectly. The blocking was well executed, the hole was there, and he could have marched in for a touchdown."

But Spofford, instead of going out and cutting back into the line, ran directly into a pileup in the line consisting of his blocking back, guard Jac Weller, and Ben Grosscup, whose head, according to Weller, was "between my knees."

The Princeton threat was, at least temporarily, stopped.

Trying to run down the clock, Roscoe bravely (a fumble now could have been disastrous) took the ball into the line twice and picked up a few yards. In the huddle before each play, he told his team, "I'll get as far as I can, and when you see me down, everybody pile on top of me. That will eat up some time while the officials dig me out." On third down Fuller went back into the end zone to punt. The pass from center was high. Fuller juggled it, bringing it down to kick. End Gil Lea was bearing down on him. Fuller just did get it off, a low line drive that skimmed over the heads of the linemen. It was caught at the 30.

Chooch Train had charged forward untouched with the snap of the ball, ready to take aim at whoever caught it. When he saw it was Homer Spofford, into his mind popped the warning he'd been given about Spofford's great stiff-arm move. "Oh my God," he said to himself. "Here it comes." At the same time another prep school credo flashed, "Go in low and keep your feet turned."

Trying to elude the runaway Train, Spofford retreated six yards but in vain. Train went in low and wrapped his arms around Spofford's legs, and down they went. "Boy," Train said, "when I got my arms around his legs I never felt better in my life."

Princeton ran for a first down; then, with seconds remaining, three passing attempts were knocked down and the half ended.

18 | November 17, Halftime

WEARILY, THE TWO TEAMS TRUDGED UP THE RAMP AT THE
closed end of Palmer Stadium and turned in opposite directions toward the halftime rooms under the concrete structure—
for Yale the same small, hot, stuffy room they had met in before the game.

On the field both schools' bands and a color guard massed
behind the north goal posts as the public address announcer
spoke:

> You are about to participate in a ceremony dedicated to the
> memory of William Winston Roper [who had died the previ-
> ous December], continuously from the World War until 1930
> and for five years earlier coach of Princeton football squads.
> His final Yale-Princeton game, played on this field four years
> ago, contributed conclusive evidence to prove that he so in-
> stilled Princeton football teams with his own unquenchable
> spirit that they possessed a unique distinction of their own.
> ... In the brief ceremony which will begin at the conclusion of
> this announcement, Princeton today pays inadequate tribute
> to the memory of a great sportsman, a vivid and forceful per-
> sonality, its loyal son, Bill Roper.

The bands, color guard, and a bugler marched to midfield,
where they played Old Nassau, as the Princeton crowd waved
their hats side to side. The bugler played taps, the color guard
marched off the field to a drumbeat, and the bands performed
their halftime routines.

In the Princeton halftime room, there was little evidence
of unquenchable spirit. When the Tiger was rolling, Fritz Crisler had little to say at halftime.

This was not one of those times. He was nervous and tense,

and it was palpable to his players. He was aware that his team had been, as he later put it, "a little stage struck" at the start of the game.

"You better settle down and play the kind of ball you're capable of," he said, "and you can beat these guys."

He mentioned some individuals, pointing out what they could or should do better. Nothing was aimed at Pepper Constable. They all knew he was burning up inside—they could hear him raging at himself on the field when he missed a block; once when he'd fallen down on a play into the line, he had given himself the devil for not playing up to his own expectations.

The fumbles were eating at Crisler. "You've got to hold onto the ball better," he reminded them.

Mose Kalbaugh was in pain. On a play near the end of the half he had suffered a cracked vertebra, but he said nothing about it. What he did talk about was the game plan. He wanted Katz Kadlic to forget the new passing plays; they weren't working. Forget trying to confuse the Yale defense. Just ram the ball through on the 31-32-33 power plays.

Crisler tried to send them back inspired and eager to prove themselves. Writer Tim Cohane quoted Crisler as saying, "I have not the honor to be a Princeton man, so I do not feel I can intrude myself upon the sanctity of this moment. I will leave you with your thoughts. What is it to be?"

The stuffy Yale quarters were quiet, some players lying down, others sitting, heads bowed, deep in their own thoughts. As part of his usual time-out and halftime routine, Major Wandle gave Lou Walker a box of sugar cubes and a bottle of rum. "Lace these with the rum and give one to each man," Wandle told him. Some of them—Whitehead, Kelley, a few others—refused them. Once had been enough for them. Chooch Train liked them; they made him feel like a new man. Jerry Roscoe was lying on his back. He felt sick and out of breath. Lou Walker said, "Open your mouth" and dropped a sugar cube in it and he retched.

They took some water and spit it out. Wandle didn't want them drinking anything during a game, not even at halftime. He gave Kim Whitehead another shot of painkiller.

Everything was low key. There was no "win one for Pop Corbin or Pudge Heffelfinger." Ivan Williamson talked quietly to the ends, Denny Myers to the other linemen. Williamson told Train how to deal with the blocking duo.

"I can't go in there and hit that goddamn tandem," Train said. "They're coming at me bigger than hell."

Williamson said, "They ain't going to do it. You're going to knock that tandem right back in their lap. They ain't going to know what to do."

Train tried it, and they didn't run his side again.

Greasy Neale discussed the game plan with the backfield. "We can beat these guys," he said. "Just keep doing what you've been doing."

Somebody wondered aloud, "How long can these guys go on this way?"

Major Wandle said, "Don't worry about them. They can handle themselves. They're all in great condition."

19 | November 17, Third Quarter

THE PRINCETON ELEVEN CAME OUT FOR THE SECOND HALF looking fired up with renewed determination.

Hugh MacMillan kicked off, and Jerry Roscoe made the same mistake Ken Sandbach had made at the start of the game. He fumbled the ball; it rolled into the end zone; instead of downing it, he picked it up and made it out to the 10-yard line. The Bulldogs wasted no time getting out of there. On second down

Fuller punted low and away from LeVan, and the ball rolled and rolled and finally stopped after a 72-yard journey to the Princeton 28.

Katz Kadlic went back to the ground game. With Kaufman and Constable pounding the line and LeVan sweeping around the outside, they covered 6, 8, up to 19 yards at a time. It took them just six plays to reach the Yale 12. Once again the orange-and-black students and fans were rocking and roaring. They sent up a cheer when LeVan scrambled for 5 yards to the 7, then were becalmed when three blue-shirts broke into the backfield on a lateral play and threw Les Kaufman for a 3-yard loss. Bypassing Constable, Kadlic called for LeVan to throw a pass into the end zone. Stan Fuller almost intercepted it but dropped it. Still ignoring what had brought the Tigers this close, Kadlic passed again to MacMillan deep in the end zone. This one was caught as the crowd rose to its feet screaming in glee. But the Yale defenders had forced MacMillan to back up six inches beyond the end zone to make the catch and the cheers quickly subsided.

This fourth-down incomplete pass into the end zone turned the ball over to Yale at the 20.

After three plays gained 8 yards, Fuller punted. This time LeVan caught it. He headed for the sideline as Train and Kelley and Whitehead led the charge at him. Train saw LeVan was going to step out of bounds and figured he'd "give him a good lick while he was doing it." Game accounts say LeVan fumbled the ball and it rolled out of bounds, but it's unclear if he dropped it before Train hit him and they were both chasing the ball or after Train hit him. Either way, Train whammed into him at full speed at a forty-five-degree angle, and, taking the head linesman, L. A. Young, with them, they all went flying across the Yale bench, sending scrubs scattering in all directions. A loud crack was heard as LeVan's ribs crashed into the bench. Whitehead thought it was the end of Train for the day. He bent over Chooch. Train stirred, looked at LeVan motionless on the ground.

"God damn," Train said, "that guy's hurt bad. He's in terrible shape. And I did it."

Whitehead said, "I wish you'd killed the sonofabitch."

Train was still down, trying to regain his breath. Looking down at Train, Ducky Pond told John Overall to get ready to go in. Pointing to Train, Pond asked Greasy Neale, "Shall we take him out?"

"Let him go," Neale said. "The hell with it. Let eleven men beat them."

Stan Fuller, standing nearby, didn't hear them. He was more concerned with Neale's taking him out because he'd kicked one to LeVan.

LeVan got up and stayed in the game for one play, then Pauk replaced him and he walked off the field to a loud ovation.

Train stayed in the game, to the amazement of Princeton end Gil Lea. "Train played opposite me. He was a little guy. Between plays he'd be down and looked like he could hardly get up and walk. We'd get back into position and he didn't look like he could make it. Then the ball would be snapped and he'd be right back in action."

A minute later, another collision occurred.

MacMillan sent a high punt that Roscoe waited for at the 20. Just as he caught it, Jac Weller ran into him. Weller's shoulder banged into his chest and down went Roscoe, out cold, unable to breathe. Major Wandle hurried out and revived him. Roscoe heaved and caught his breath. Ducky Pond had Tom Curtin up to go in for him. Clare Curtin didn't want his brother taking Roscoe's place. As captain, he had the right to refuse a substitute. He called a second time-out to give Roscoe time to recover and waved for Tom to sit down.

The next time Fuller punted, he felt no qualms in booting

it 62 yards to Pauk, who was no Garry LeVan. Pauk was buried by blue-shirts where he caught it.

And the next time MacMillan punted, four plays later, Strat Morton took care of Jac Weller, and Roscoe ran it back to midfield. From there both sides continued the kicking game. Now in position to aim for the sidelines, Fuller put one out at the Princeton 22. The Princeton attack was sputtering. MacMillan kicked again and, after a Roscoe to Kelley pass good for 10 yards, the third quarter ended on the Princeton 36, second and 8.

By this time, two rising tides—one of confidence, one of frustration—were becoming evident on the field and in the stands. Led by captain Clare Curtin's example of determination and fierce attacking, the Yale line was outplaying Princeton's.

Curtin and Scott worked together on offense. "We would talk it over going up to the line," Scott said, "who would hit our target high and who would hit him low. Or if we knew we could do it, we'd put our shoulders into him and carry him into the linebacker and get him too."

Jac Weller had been trap blocked six times, the first game in which he had ever been trapped.

Larry Kelley said, "The feeling came on us: hey, these guys are not going to score on us. We've got this ball game."

Ben Grosscup was thinking the same way: "They began to think they were going to lose and we had them."

Chooch Train said, "We weren't playing over our heads. We were used to being in close, tough games and getting beat up on and Princeton wasn't. They were dumbstruck from the start, then they couldn't move. Then they got the idea that nothing they did was right." The Bulldogs were, as actor Lionel Barrymore said of actors, *en flammes*, inflamed with their particular role in this time and place, one they would never be able to reproduce.

Gil Lea confirmed that Train was reading them right. "I felt frustrated and disjointed. We had not been pushed like they were pushing us. They were throwing us off balance. Our timing was off. We had underestimated Yale. They were marvelous, playing the game of their lives."

Ben Delaney said, "We were discouraged and mystified. We didn't stay with the running game which was working."

Katz Kadlic seemed befuddled. It was as though he felt compelled to stay with the new passing plays Fritz Crisler had given them for the game, even though they weren't working. And there was no way to confer with the coach during a time-out.

By this time any tension the Bulldogs may have felt earlier had disappeared. They were loose, busting with confidence, enjoying themselves. Jimmy DeAngelis said, "One assignment I loved. The Kaufman brothers were from West Haven, in the shadow of Yale, but they went to Princeton. When MacMillan went back to punt, three of us keyed on Les Kaufman. First Kelley was to hit him and slow him up. Then I was to hit him. Then Whitehead hit him. We hit him all the way down the field. We had a lot of fun harassing him down the field."

20 | November 17, Fourth Quarter

FACING THE OPEN END OF THE STADIUM, ROSCOE OPENED the fourth quarter by completing a pass to Kelley over the middle for a first down on the Princeton 24. Failing to move the ball, he called for a field goal attempt. A 10-point lead would give them a safety factor. On the sidelines, Greasy Neale looked on, imperceptibly in agreement with the call. Clare Curtin's place-kick from the 35 was short and wide.

Starting on their 20, with Garry LeVan back in the game and plenty of time, the Tigers inexplicably kicked on first down. Roscoe signaled for a fair catch at his own 39. A pass to Train netted a first down. After three plays got them nowhere, Fuller was in position to aim for the coffin corner again. He missed. Not only did he miss, but he also kicked it where LeVan could catch it on the goal line. Led by Hugh MacMillan, who took out two would-be tacklers, LeVan tore up the sideline as hearts leapt and stopped and thumped on the Yale sidelines until a swarm of Bulldogs stopped him near the 40.

Stan Fuller was looking over his shoulder, expecting Greasy Neale to send in somebody to take his place. Nobody got up.

On the first play, Kadlic went into the bag of tricks, a reverse to MacMillan, who was supposed to throw a pass. His effort was a soft, wobbling pass that fell into Fuller's hands. He raced 14 yards with it before LeVan tackled him. "That makes up for that kick to LeVan," Fuller sighed.

More concerned with gaining seconds off the clock than yards on the ground, Roscoe sent Morton and Fuller into the line for three plays. Fuller then aimed for the corner, and this time he nailed it—out at the 2-yard line. Princeton was right back where they had started the game. And they did what they had done then, MacMillan kicking on first down from deep in the end zone.

Roscoe caught it at the 38. Taking their time in the huddles and watching the clock, Yale ran three more plays into the line. Then Fuller kicked again. This one went out of bounds at the 3.

"It was a pretty hopeless feeling seeing those punts go out inside the five," said Gil Lea.

Once again MacMillan kicked it out of the end zone on first down. The sideline quarterbacks in the concrete horseshoe scratched their heads, wondering why Princeton was playing what appeared to be a defensive game when it trailed 7–0 and time was getting short. Later Ken Sandbach said, "I suppose Kadlic thought of the quick kick as an offensive weapon, to move the ball a lot of yards in a hurry and count on a fumble or some error to give us good field position."

It didn't work. Roscoe's punt return style was to decoy the charging defenders by standing a few yards back from where the ball would come down, then dashing forward to catch it on the run and sprinting toward an opening. This time he ran it back to the 25.

Right guard Dick John was another Tiger seething with frustration. Ben Grosscup said, "I was playing against him and knocking him on his tail all day and he finally started slugging me when he was on defense."

This feud almost led to a Yale substitution. Later field judge Jim Keegan was asked if the game had been rough. "No, not rough," he said. "Hard, but not rough. There were just two fellows, one on each side, who got a little hot-tempered. Each one accused the other of starting it. Umpire Tom Thorp warned them he'd have to run them off the field if they kept it up, and that cooled them out."

Keegan wouldn't name names, but Grosscup and John were the only two whose actions fit the description.

Now John boiled over, but Grosscup wasn't involved. Kim Whitehead was stopped at the line for no gain. He was sitting on the ground when John lunged at him and hit him with a fist. Everybody in Palmer Stadium saw it.

The 15-yard penalty put Yale at the 10. Three plays into the line gained 3. Fourth down at the 7. One minute to play. Roscoe thought: field goal, a chip shot, an easy 3 points. As they lined up for the kick, Greasy Neale's innards tightened. He was having a silent, invisible fit. A blocked kick, he thought, and then an open field for a touchdown run, at best a recovery way up field somewhere with a minute left for Princeton to score. Do nothing, Roscoe. Fall on the ball, and they'll have it on the 7. But Neale was powerless to intervene. Even if he could call time and send in a sub, the man was not allowed to say a word before a play was run.

And there was no certainty about the time left. Unknown to the players and coaches, the big clock they were watching had been as much as forty seconds off one way or the other at times during the day.

Princeton left tackle Bob Kopf was thinking the same thing: block that kick. The ball was snapped. Roscoe knelt and held it. Kopf faked a blocker and rushed in as Curtin kicked. Kopf could feel the wind of the ball going by his fingertips. Only a harness strapped to an injured shoulder had prevented him from reaching as far as he normally could.

The kick was wide. Greasy Neale couldn't care less. He relaxed—a little.

As Princeton huddled, Larry Kelley loudly counted down the seconds. On his own 20 with a minute to play, Kadlic turned their failed passing attack over to Ken Sandbach. The first attempt was knocked down by Stan Fuller. The second was intercepted at the 31 by Kim Whitehead. Jerry Roscoe let the clock run out, and Yale had scored the greatest upset in its long football tradition.

Princeton had gained 167 yards on the ground, Yale 67. All of Princeton's 7 first downs were on the ground; all of Yale's 4 were through the air. Princeton's passing game had failed miserably: 2 for 14 total, 0 for 6 in the second half, with two interceptions in the fourth quarter alone.

In the fourth quarter Princeton had had the ball for six plays: 3 first-down punts, 3 passes, 2 intercepted. Not a single running play. Yale had run 27 plays.

21 | November 17, Post-Game

TWENTY-TWO DAZED YOUNG MEN STOOD IN THE CENTER OF a swirling, cheering, yelling, scrambling, running mob at 4:20 p.m. on the field in Palmer Stadium. The men in orange and black were in a state of shock, disbelief, and embarrassment that they had been beaten by a team that, man-to-man, they clearly outclassed. The men in blue, as drained as a beer keg at a frat party, were too numb, confused, and bone-weary to even think about doing any celebrating. Some of them had lost ten pounds or more during the game.

Not so the thousands of Yale rooters, some of whom attacked both goal posts. The posts were made of steel and embedded in concrete; that didn't stop the exuberant mob. They tore down both of them, then attacked the big clock at the south end and splintered it into pieces they could carry off for souvenirs. Others swarmed around the victorious Yale eleven, pounding them on the back as they tried to make their way through the open end of the stadium to the dressing room.

The Yale band marched zigzag down the field, leading a noisy snake dance of students, alumni, girlfriends, and wives. (At the same time in New York City, a brass band was leading a raucous column of alums from the Yale Club down Park Avenue to the Princeton Club, singing "Boola," "Bingo," and "Down the Field.")

The Princeton fans stood where they had sat for two hours, in stunned, disbelieving silence, watching the madness. It was at least fifteen minutes before most of them stirred and started moving toward the exits.

Jimmy DeAngelis clutched the game ball to his chest, trying to swerve and dodge the growing human maelstrom around him so nobody would take it from him. When he slowed to a walk, somebody grabbed his helmet and ran off with it. It turned out to be a friend, who returned it to him the next week.

For DeAngelis, the sweetness of victory was tinged with sadness. Some of the players had family members there who came down on the field to share the moment with their sons and brothers. He had no one; his family didn't care about football.

Stan Fuller lost his helmet too: "I was carrying it and it was usual for the equipment people to come out on the field and take it to get started packing, so when it left my hand I wasn't surprised. The next week I got a letter from the thief saying he was the captain of his team now because he was the only one who had a helmet. I never got it back."

Kim Whitehead was numb, physically and mentally, limping on his torn-up knee in what felt like a trance.

Meredith Scott, normally unmoved to any emotional outburst, win or lose, stood absorbing the pushing and pounding, disoriented and sobbing. He grabbed a stranger by the sleeve and said, "How do I get out of here?" The nearest way out was through the closed end. The stranger led Scott through the tunnel beneath the stadium around to the other end and toward the field house.

Larry Kelley needed help too. Physically, mentally, and emotionally exhausted, he didn't know what to do or where to go. He saw somebody he knew, his prep school roommate, Jack Sergeant. Sergeant held him up on one side and somebody he didn't know held him on the other side and they started out. But they took a wrong turn and wound up under the stands in the deserted halftime room before they found the way out.

Ben Grosscup went back to the stuffy little room too, looking for somebody to give him a rubdown.

In the press box, amid the chattering typewriters and Western Union keys, writers ran through their fields of vocabulary, dodging cliches, stiff-arming the unrelenting clock of early editions, trying to describe what they had witnessed. The more experienced among them went back to 1925 to recall the last time a favored Princeton team had been upset, and then it had been Yale that stopped them, 10–0, a week after Princeton had smothered Harvard, 34–0. But even those veterans seemed stumped for a way to sum up this game in the brief, pointed kind of lead they teach in journalism school.

Stanley Woodward's lead for the *New York Herald-Tribune* waxed on for seventy-seven words in two sentences: "Eleven Yale football players with constitutions of iron and dispositions of wild cats perpetrated the signal outrage of modern athletics in Princeton's Palmer Stadium today. Overmanned by the proud power of Old Nassau, rated as forlorn and hopeless candidates for second place at odds ranging up to 4 to 1, these intractable sons of Elihu Yale rose on their legs and beat Princeton's unbeatables, 7–0."

Readers across the country dependent on wire service reports saw the first use of the phrase "iron men of Yale" in the dispatch from Associated Press sports editor Alan Gould: "Eleven stalwarts in blue, eleven 'iron men' of Yale who laughed at the odds and the opposition against them, rose to magnificent heights of gridiron achievement today and swept Princeton from the ranks of the nation's unbeaten teams in the most spectacular upset of the 1934 football season."

Robert F. Kelley of the *New York Times* pecked out, "Yale defeated Princeton today by a score of 7–0. In that sentence is packed all the deep excitement of the most popular drama that football or any other sport knows—the rise of the man without a chance, the refusal of the underdog to play the role that has been assigned to him. The Tiger found for the first time this year a line that carried the fight to it and a team which absolutely refused to yield an inch."

Kelley and other writers credited Stan Fuller's fourth-quarter coffin-nailing punting with sealing the victory. Among the losers, Garry LeVan was singled out. He had run like a fiend, blocked viciously, and tackled flawlessly.

The next day, given time to digest what he had seen, Kelley wrote, "Not often in the long history of football has a team been brought to a big game tuned as the maestro tunes a violin."

Greasy Neale went on to win NFL championships with the Philadelphia Eagles and a place in the pro football Hall of Fame, but nothing matched his tuning of those eleven young men in blue for this one game.

Perhaps no one in Palmer Stadium that day had watched the action more intently than the Harvard scouts, assistant coach Adam Walsh and athletic director Bill Bingham. In a story for the *Boston Post* Walsh wrote the following:

> Mental attitude means much to a football team. Yale had 11 men keyed to a high pitch and Princeton didn't, and that is the answer to the biggest upset of this hectic season. As strange as it may seem, Princeton never had a chance against those 11 smart, hard-fighting boys of Yale. Right from the opening kick-off you could see that this Yale team was out for blood, and blood they got in the pay-off.
>
> Yale's running game was only a threat, but a threat is all you need when you have such a fine passer as Jerry Roscoe and a fellow like this wildman Kelley. Kelley handles that ball with one hand as a baseball player would handle a baseball. Roscoe and Kelley put on as fine an exhibition of passing and receiving as you will ever witness. Jerry's passes were perfect and Larry's receiving was remarkable. And maybe you think this boy Kelley doesn't know what to do when he gets the ball in his hand. After making a fine catch he ran the ball like a halfback and over the line he went, standing up.

The phrase "Iron Men of Yale" began to appear in stories and headlines. It was not unheard of for eleven men to play an entire game. Greasy Neale's 1922 Rose Bowl team, Washington & Jefferson, had done it. Army had done it during Major Wandle's time there. A Brown team had done it twice in 1926.

Nobody realized at the time that they had just seen it done for the last time.

There was nothing subdued about the Yale dressing room. A full-scale celebration was going on. Old grads and undergrads; football heroes of the past, including Ted Coy, Tad Jones, Pie Way, and Johnny Kilpatrick; people they all knew and people nobody knew were there to greet the weary players as they straggled in.

Bob Hall came in and he and Stan Fuller gave each other a bear hug. "If you had gone to Princeton," Hall said, "Yale wouldn't have won today."

Forty years later Fuller wrote to Jimmy DeAngelis, "Bob Hall should be honored as the twelfth man on the November 17, 1934, team. I bowed out with three broken ribs in the Yale freshmen–Roxbury game the year he coached me in 1930. He encouraged me not to give up my determination to get to Yale while I detoured via Ohio University. He was sympathetic during my first-year transfer of ineligibility, and disappointments in my junior year from a pulled hamstring followed by a bone growth that sidelined me for the rest of the season. Any wonder that I bear-hugged him when he ran into the Palmer Stadium locker room after the final gun."

In the locker room somebody mentioned that only eleven men had played that day for Yale. Although Roscoe and Whitehead had said something between them late in the game about no subs being used, it was the first time the others realized it. They had been too busy concentrating on the job at hand to notice it. It didn't sink in for some of them until they were on the train to New York.

John Hersey was one of the reserves on the bench that afternoon. Fifty years later he was asked for his impressions of the eleven Iron Men. This is what he wrote:

Clare Curtin: stolid, silent, sober, and immovable.

Choo-Choo (or "Chooch") Train: wonderfully bow-legged, incredibly brave, a Georgian with a sardonic humor, cheerful, aggressive on the field without any anger, a great end.

Larry Kelley: an even greater end. Larry had a marked distaste for physical contact, and he was agile. Thus, no one ever touched him. Even on offense, he did more by head fakes and little dance steps that fooled the opponent than by use of his shoulders. Marvelous hands; he could catch a pass with one finger. A sarcastic tongue—he talked himself into the Princeton backfield on defense that day.

Meredith Scott: big for those days, weighed 220, would be disqualified from major teams these days because too small.

Jimmy DeAngelis: a New Haven townie, an angelic man, kind and considerate. Tiny for a guard.

Ben Grosscup: another southerner with a face that would frighten the opponents, as tease great fun, very tough on the field.

Jerry Roscoe: a gentleman scholar, handsome, rather quiet, well-mannered, unflappable.

Kim Whitehead: taciturn, quick to flare, with amazing endurance, captain the next year.

Stan Fuller: Reddish complexion, silent, sturdy. He won the game, in my opinion, with his kicks that rolled dead or went out of bounds within the five yard line time and again.

Jack Wright: big, black-haired, fair-skinned, very good-natured and fun to be around.

Strat Morton: another small-bodied but huge-hearted guy, with another sassy tongue which confused the Tigers.

Hersey added, "Football was a test of spirit when players went both ways, and of course spirit won that game. Did the others tell you how the hordes of great Princetons, who had gone undefeated for ages (with the help of some we considered ringers from Kiski Academy—was it?), lined up along their sideline before the game while we were warming up, all with their arms with gold stripes on them folded in a show of utter contempt for our ragamuffin squad? That was a bad mistake. It may have lost the game."

Inside the Princeton dressing room there was silence, the silence of complete depression. It was Fritz Crisler's first loss at Palmer Stadium since his arrival in 1932 and the first loss ever for those who had starred on the '32 freshman team.

Fritz Crisler said, "We lost a ball game we shouldn't have lost," and that was it.

But outside the dressing room there was fury.

"You can't imagine the furor that was created by our losing this game," said Gil Lea, "among alumni, friends, everyone. They came to the field house where we were dressing and they were furious with us. The feeling was so intense, we were shunned on campus the next week. Even one of the janitors in a building wouldn't talk to me for a week."

The next day three members of the team went to New York. They dropped in at the Princeton Club. Ben Delaney said, "One of us asked an old alum there for a nickel to call a friend. The man said, 'Here's two nickels. Call all of them.'"

On Saturday night the bell atop Nassau Hall, which pealed when Princeton won the Big 3 title, was silent. The fences that had been marked for sacrifice on the victory bonfire remained standing. There was little gaiety among those who showed up for Hildebrecht's anticipated celebration special $1.25 Surf Club dinner.

"A shroud of stunned disbelief enveloped the campus on which is buried the late regretted undefeated Princeton Tiger," mourned the *Trenton Times*.

For the first time ever after a home game, the Tigers were loaded onto buses at the field house and taken out of town, back to the same Lawrenceville dorm they had occupied the night before the game. They didn't even have a chance to see their families. Before they left, Crisler told reporters, "I was especially impressed with the effectiveness of the Roscoe-Kelley pass combination. But the rugged Yale line gave a grand exhibition too."

Tired as they were, that night the Princeton men couldn't sleep. Gradually they emerged from their rooms and gathered in the hall, sitting with their backs to the wall, blankets over their shoulders, like a line of ghosts, till one o'clock, then two o'clock, bemoaning, rehashing, second-guessing. It was only then that they realized they had been beaten by just eleven men.

Had they been overconfident, or had they just underestimated Yale? And where was the line between the two?

"How could we have lost to *that* team. . . . We have so much talent. . . . We could have run any one of our three backfield units out there and won. . . . What went wrong? . . . Maybe we did have an easier schedule than they did, but we're still better than they are. . . . Wait till next year. . . . Yeah, next time we play them, every time we see a Yalie standing up, we'll knock the sonofabitch down no matter where he is on the field. . . ."

There was no blame-casting, no name calling. They knew they had all fallen flat, been outfought and outplayed. Each one had his own failings to deal with—the fumbles, the missed blocks and tackles, the errant timing. They couldn't bring themselves to admit that if they hadn't played their game, it was because those eleven Bulldogs from Yale didn't let them.

Later the undergrads would realize that they had gained some poise and an ability to deal with adversity that would prove valuable in building a new winning streak. But for now that was no consolation.

Katz Kadlic, whose play calling would be second-guessed whenever this game was talked about, was inconsolable. His mother had never seen him play, and his whole family had come up from West Virginia for the game. *That* game.

Nobody even tried to console Pepper Constable. They knew he was silently beating up on himself more severely than any of them could have done to themselves and survived.

The Yale Athletic Association had planned a night out in New York, win or lose, for the Bulldogs: dinner on the train; tickets to the hit Broadway musical at the Winter Garden, *Life Begins at 8:40*, starring Bert Lahr and Ray Bolger; rooms at the Hotel New Yorker.

Training rules were relaxed in their private car to New York. They could smoke, drink a few beers. For a few of the exhausted players, a few beers were enough to get them feeling giddy.

Old Yale grad Rudy Vallee had a nightclub in New York, with a standing invitation to Yale football players to be his guests any time. Stan Fuller and a few others went there before the show.

Some of them skipped the show. Kim Whitehead and his roommate, Dick Barr, went to Plainfield, New Jersey, to spend the night at his parents' home. Whitehead was in so much pain, he went to see an osteopath for a rubdown and massage.

Jerry Roscoe was too emotionally and physically drained to sit through a show. Exhausted, he went to bed early, but he was so wound up he barely slept two hours.

Bob Train's parents were there, so he spent the evening with them.

Some of those who went to the show didn't see much of it. Larry Kelley and Jimmy DeAngelis were there but fell asleep. Kelley usually had trouble sleeping the night after a game, but he was completely drained. "They told me it was a wonderful show," DeAngelis said.

Some who didn't fall asleep wished they had. Ben Grosscup said, "I was a rugged mountaineer, but I was absolutely exhausted and sore all over. That musical was the most painful thing I ever sat through."

Their itinerary called for lights out fifteen minutes after returning from the show. Nobody needed that reminder except the student managers, who had ordered champagne in their rooms, courtesy of the wager winners, Pat Garvan and Lou Walker. The $2,500 Walker would collect on Monday would be the biggest bet he'd ever win.

On Sunday the coaches remained in New York to watch the Chicago Bears play the New York Giants at the Polo Grounds. There was still the Harvard game ahead of them. Greasy Neale would be looking for a new play he could use.

The players were called for breakfast at 9:00 a.m. in a private dining room. Buses took them to Grand Central Station to catch the eleven o'clock train to New Haven, where they were treated to lunch in the Ray Tompkins House Grille.

Back in his room on Sunday afternoon, Stan Fuller, known as "Bud" to his family, wrote a letter home. His father had listened to the game back in Erie, his ear pressed against the radio for two hours to make out every play in the faint, crackling broadcast. Fuller's mother thought he would have a heart attack before it was over. The letter gives a hint of what it was like to be a football player and student of limited means at Yale in 1934:

Dear Folks,

Well, by this time you have read a full account of the game, and there isn't much that I can add to that. The very fact that the team that started played the entire game is saying enough about the game right there. We went out there to win, and not just to hold them down. We felt that we had a chance, and we were right. I was never so tired and happy at the same time. Jack was there after the game, and so were Lovdie and Virginia, with Lovdie's uncle. Needless to say, they enjoyed the game.

We spent the night in New York, at the Hotel New Yorker, which is quite a swanky place, by the way. Last night the A.A. took us to see the musical comedy "Life Begins at 8:40." It was some fun, starring Bert Lahr, and several other Broadway favorites whom I never heard of before.

I don't believe I ever received so many telegrams in my life as I have yesterday and today. There were eight or nine of them; from Uncle John, some friends of his in Erie, you, the Welshes, and several others whom I don't recall having had the pleasure of meeting. And speaking of Uncle John. I think he was there yesterday, but evidently he wasn't in shape to see me, because the first I heard from him was the telegram which I mentioned, congratulating me and asking me to get four tickets for the Harvard game this week for him. I don't know whether or not I'll be able to do that or not, because four tickets at 3.85 apiece runs into more money than I have at the moment.

Another item of importance: I found in the mail today a notice that my subscription to the Gazette and Bulletin had run its full course, and was now in a state of decadence, which could only be remedied by an addition to the principle. Will you be obliging and remedy that, because I don't know what I should do without my daily paper from home.

I'm still tired from that ball game. Of course I haven't slept any too well in the last two days, what with running around the country, but I'll soon enough make up for it. It's nearly three o'clock now, and when I finish this I shall sleep until supper time.

It is just like summer out today. Even a coat and vest are warm, and it is an atmosphere very conducive to sleep. And to think that just this past Wednesday and Thursday it was so cold we almost froze during practice, especially when the wind would sweep across the field at fifty miles an hour. I hope the mild weather keeps up until after the Harvard game, and then I don't care how cold it does get. From that time on, until spring, everything will be held indoors, and there is positive assurance of enough heat to keep everyone warm then.

Now I think I'll go shave and then sleep. I believe that the last chance I had to shave was Thursday night, and this is Sunday, so you can imagine how much I am in need of one right now.

Only a few more weeks until Christmas Vacation, and a complete rest.

Your son,
Bud

Given a few days to reflect on what they had witnessed, the New York writers were asked by the editor of the *Yale Daily News* for their reactions to the game.

Stanley Woodward responded, "What can I say? The game the Yale team played Saturday was an impossibility. It couldn't have happened. I've never seen anything like it."

Will B. Johnstone of the *World-Telegram*: "I have been covering football since Ted Coy's day and never have I seen a Yale team put on a greater defensive exhibition than I did on Saturday. Yale was in perfect condition, like a winning prizefighter who has had some tough battles instead of a lot of set-ups. It was the suicide schedule that put Yale in condition and enabled the Blue team to win."

Lawrence Perry, *New York Sun*: "Yale's defensive exhibition was remarkable, really stunning. Princeton, of course, was tighter than a bowstring at the start and the mishandling of the kick-off put the team off. Princeton tried to gain by splitting the Yale line, as Army and Georgia did, but this time Yale's defense left nothing to be desired."

Robert F. Kelley of the *Times*: "In response to your request for comment on the Yale-Princeton game, I would like to say that the first reaction I had was one of gratitude that I had been able to see the game. It was certainly one which will be remembered for a great many years by any of the people who saw it, one worthy in every respect of the high tradition of this series. It was also an intensely valuable game, in that it served to remind a good many people, who were apparently in danger of forgetting the fact, that football's best attribute is the creation of and continuance of games of this nature, in which it is almost utterly impossible to pick the winner before the start."

Pat Robinson, International News Service: "Yale outsmarted Princeton from beginning to end. Roscoe's field generalship was unsurpassed by any other quarterback this year. The end play of Train and Kelley left nothing to be desired, and Fuller's sensational punting kept the Tigers back on their heels. Yale was a 1–5 shot before the game but they finished like a 10–1 shot."

22 | November 24

AS HE BEGAN TO PREPARE HIS TEAM FOR THE LAST GAME of the 1934 season and the start of a new winning streak, Fritz Crisler said, "As the game went Saturday, Princeton was beaten fairly and squarely by a superior team. We got off to a poor start and the whole eleven acted as though it were stagestruck, just as it did against Washington and Lee. Yale put on an extremely valiant fight to score an upset and it did this by sweeping us off our feet. I thought the passing combination of Roscoe and Kelley was as fine as I have seen this year. There is one consolation, however, and that is that the whole squad will be in a better frame of mind for the Dartmouth game."

On Monday Crisler saw a team that was on edge, physically and emotionally. It was difficult to tell if the players would be pressing in the Dartmouth game, overanxious maybe to make up for their performance against Yale. He decided to ease up on the scrimmaging for the week.

The experts had become skittish about picking winners. Predictions for next Saturday's action had more hedges than the English countryside.

But the Tigers had come out of their adverse experience with more poise and determination. They scored twice in the first quarter against Dartmouth and three more times in the second, then sent in armies of subs for the rest of their 38–13 season-ending victory. It was the start of a new twelve-game winning streak.

On December 3 at the annual Princeton football dinner at the Princeton Inn, Katz Kadlic was awarded the John Prentiss Poe cup. The award, given in the name of a Princeton football star killed in the Great War, went to the man who exemplified best the traits of "loyalty, courage, manliness, self-control, modesty, and perseverance."

The players elected Pepper Constable 1935 captain, the first back to win the honor since 1921.

Stan Fuller was the first of the eleven Yale starters in Saturday's game to arrive for practice Monday afternoon. He was greeted by Hokus, the Spalding equipment man. "There's a fellow out on the practice field who wants to see you," he said. Fuller dressed and went out. He saw a man of about sixty-five standing at the 50-yard line. He approached and said, "I'm Stan Fuller. Did you want to see me?"

"Yes," the man said, holding out his hand. "I'm Pop Corbin. I was captain of the first iron man team in 1888. I just want to say bully for you."

Corbin stayed there until the other ten came out to see him.

Other old-timers, including former coaches Jack Owsley and Ralph Bloomer, were there as well. They reminisced with Corbin, whose 1888 team had played thirteen games, won them all, and outscored its opponents, 698–0. The team had played without subs in nine games. "Twice we lost a man to injury," Corbin said, "and twice because of a major rule violation by a player."

An unusually large number of students showed up to watch the practice sessions that week. They didn't see much on Monday; the "Iron Men" were still too weary to exert themselves, and little was asked of them. Mentally and emotionally the Bulldogs had closed their season with the victory at Princeton. They didn't expect Harvard to give them as tough a battle as the other seven games on their schedule. The coaches had to exert a little push to get them ready.

Thursday's practice in the Bowl was open to the public. The brass band played Yale battle songs and was joined by several hundred singing students.

Enthusiasm ran high for this fifty-third meeting of Yale and

Harvard. Twenty-two special trains headed for New Haven from all directions. There was even a chartered yacht from the Manhasset Bay Yacht Club on Long Island. New Haven store windows were decked out in crimson and blue. Despite Harvard's 3-4 record, the wary bookies were calling the game even.

Greasy Neale came up with another new play, a fake placekick when they got within field-goal range. The snap would go to Roscoe, who would kneel and hold the ball for Curtin. But he was to inform the officials to notice that his knee would not touch the ground when he held the ball, which would end the play. Roscoe would then take the ball around end.

A cold rain on Friday night left a nip in the air and a strong wind on Saturday. Many among the crowd of forty-eight thousand wrapped themselves in colorful rugs and blankets. The eleven Iron Men started the game, Kim Whitehead wearing a brace made by Major Wandle to support his injured knee. Clare Curtin won the coin toss but did not elect to kick off as he usually did. He used his option by choosing to defend the north goal and start with the wind at his back. It was a good decision. Harvard kicked off.

Aided by the tailwind, Stan Fuller won the early kicking game. After Yale's first drive was stopped at the Harvard 28, the Crimson moved the ball to the Yale 35, where a punt put the Elis inside their own 10. Fuller then booted one that went through the air and on the ground for 68 yards. The return punt went to Yale's 40.

Roscoe's aerial circus went into action, connecting to Kelley over the middle to the Harvard 42, then to Morton for another 7. Roscoe then went through a big hole opened by Fuller and Scott on the left side to the 24. On fourth down and 4 on the Harvard 18, a strong tailwind, only a slight angle to the goal posts, it was a typical position to call a field goal. So Harvard had no reason to expect anything else when Curtin went back to the

30 and Roscoe lined up to take the snap for the placement attempt. Roscoe told the official to watch his knee, which would not touch the ground. He took the snap. Curtin went through the kicking motion. The entire Harvard line rushed in to block it. Roscoe jumped up and raced around left end and was down to the 3 when a Harvard man reached him. Roscoe went to stiffarm him; the defender lunged and grabbed just enough of his jersey to cause the ball to pop out. Harvard recovered it on the 1. The play had worked perfectly but ended for Roscoe in the most disappointing moment of his football career.

Haley of Harvard kicked into the wind out of the end zone to the 29; Roscoe returned it to the 22. Morton took a shovel pass from Roscoe and tore through the Harvard secondary to score.

Late in the quarter, Richard Crampton replaced Jack Wright at right tackle, ending the Iron Men's run of playing time as an unbroken unit.

After an exchange of punts in the second quarter, Roscoe intercepted a pass near midfield and ran it back 12 yards. Morton and Rankin, in for Kim Whitehead, carried the Bulldogs to the 7. On third down, Roscoe and Kelley teamed up again. With two men sticking close to him, Kelley slowed, then put on a burst of speed and headed for the left corner of the end zone. Roscoe lobbed it high and Kelley brought it down, tiptoeing a few steps before going out of bounds.

Just before the half ended, Stan Fuller was hurt on the runback of his 40-yard punt. The crowd stood and cheered him as he left the game. The ovation was a touching valedictory to the man from Erie, who had taken the longest, most tortuous journey of anyone on the field that afternoon before finally fulfilling his dreams and expectations. He had played his last minute for Yale.

The second half was played almost entirely in Yale's backyard as the scrappy Harvards refused to give up. Three times the Yale defense stopped them near the goal line, once when Larry Kelley raced into their backfield and broke up a statue of liberty play.

Train, DeAngelis, Kelley—all of them, without exception—played the same impenetrable defense that had become their trademark. It had been years since a Yale team had come together with as much spirit and zeal. Jerry Roscoe demonstrated that he may have been the most underrated quarterback in the country, at a time when the quarterback called all the plays and was expected to block, pass, run, play the safety position, and run back punts. As a caller of plays and an inspiring team leader, he was unexcelled. He was a better passer, punt returner, and runner from scrimmage than most, though not an exceptional blocker.

Scott and Curtin played the full sixty minutes. Several others came out a few minutes short of sixty to permit others to get into the game for at least one play, thus making them eligible to take part in electing next year's captain. (Only those who played in the Princeton or Harvard game were eligible to vote.) Twenty-three men had gotten into the game. One of them was John Hersey, who went in for Larry Kelley with one minute to play.

For the year, Ben Grosscup led them all in playing time—470 of the total 480 minutes of game time.

When the game ended, 14–0, the home crowd swarmed onto the field and tore down the goal posts at both ends of the field, while Clare Curtin and the Harvard captain, Herman Gundlach, quietly shook hands as the players headed for the dressing rooms, some of them for the last time.

On Monday, November 26, at a meeting in the Ray Tompkins lounge, Kim Whitehead was elected captain of the 1935 team. John F. Byers Jr., an assistant manager, was promoted to manager, with Frederick H. Brooke his assistant. Everybody then adjourned to the Fence Club, housed in the former Phi Epsilon frat house, for the traditional year-end football banquet. A magnum of champagne sat on the table beside each of the Iron Men, courtesy of student manager Pat Garvan's winnings on the Princeton game.

Garvan presided over the program. There were informal remarks by Malcolm Farmer, chairman of athletics; Kim Whitehead; Ducky Pond; Greasy Neale; Denny Myers; Ivan Williamson; jayvee coaches Stewart Scott, Century Milstead, and Walter Levering; freshman coach Reg Root; Major Wandle; and Clare Curtin.

Farmer said, "There has never been a football team which could compare with this one. I was all in dutch over the schedule that I made, but this team knocked it for a loop."

Farmer then lauded Pond for doing an outstanding job "because he had faith in the team and the full support of all the coaching staff."

Pointing to a large tiger skin that had been hung in the dining hall, he said it represented "a souvenir of this fine spirit which pervaded the football squad and coaches, and which was the old Yale spirit."

Kim Whitehead said, "Not enough credit could go to Pond and Greasy Neale. The greatest part of our victories was due to the deceptive plays that they showed us." He ended by saying that next year's schedule would be tough, but by following the fine example set by Clare Curtin, they would have a successful season.

Greasy Neale commented on the players: "DeAngelis put everything into his game. . . . Whitehead not only kicks the ball but makes the tackle. . . . Jerry Roscoe I think is the best quarterback in America. . . . Stan Fuller has done more for the team than almost anyone, blocking, tackling, and punting."

Major Wandle said, "I thought that nowhere would I find

the spirit that exists at West Point, but this team had every bit as fine a determination. Nowhere have I ever enjoyed myself more. This is the greatest bunch of kids I ever handled."

Ivan Williamson said the cooperation the team gave the coaches was all that could be desired.

Denny Myers said the grit and determination the team showed could have beaten the world.

Scott, the jayvee coach, then read a lengthy poetic salute to the team and the Iron Men that ended with

> So among Yale's greatest captains, Clare Curtin takes
> his place,
> His leadership will e'er inspire us when strong opponents
> must be faced.
> So we acclaim these men of iron, and to their courage
> hail,
> They are true and noble warriors who wore the blue
> of Yale.

After cheers for Curtin and Pond, they all, well lubricated by the champagne, sang loudly and somewhat off-key the school's traditional but unofficial Alma Mater, "Bright College Years," ringing down the curtain on their unforgettable football season and the evening's festivities with the rousing closing lines:

> Oh let us strive that ever we
> May let these words our watch-cry be,
> Where'er upon life's sea we sail:
> For God, for Country, and for Yale."

23 | The Rest of the Story

THE EVENTS OF THE AFTERNOON OF NOVEMBER 17, 1934, remained a part of the lives of all those who were involved in that game. For the Princeton juniors, it was to be the only game they would lose in four years as members of the freshman and varsity teams.

End Hugh MacMillan said, "I never played in another loss for Princeton. We had sixteen wins and a tie before November 17, 1934, and won twelve straight after that, but I never dream about any other game."

Garry LeVan settled in Titusville, Pennsylvania. Once when he attended a Princeton-Yale-Harvard picnic in Erie, he met Stan Fuller there. LeVan said, "Damn you, you wouldn't give me the ball that day. We won every game for three years but that one, and to this day, whenever I meet anyone from Princeton or Yale, they never mention anything about all the games we won. They only want to talk about that Yale game."

One day Fuller happened to be at the University of Michigan campus and passed Fritz Crisler going into the gym.

"I felt like going over to him and saying, 'We were on the same field one day . . .' but I didn't."

Gil Lea said the '34 team took something positive from the experience:

> The '34 team was better than the '35 team, but we had learned some poise and how to handle possible adversity from that Yale game. A lot of good came out of it for us. We experienced a maturing and growing up in that game and benefited by it in '35. We learned about ourselves and each other, how we dealt with adversity and what it did to us. We never forgot it, and it helped us in our '35 season. I have always believed that football can do a great deal for the individual, and I think

that Yale game was the most important of our career because of what it taught us. Every one of us matured in that game and it helped us in the rest of our lives.

We were very cold and calculating in '35. They had taught us a lesson. We planned a play based on the '34 game, one where we thought we would handle Mr. Kelley. We had learned that the Yale defense overreacted and all went one way after the play and if you could catch them off-balance you could score. We lined up and the play went three steps to the right, then turned around and went to the left. I at right end would sneak around and block out a back and it went for a touchdown.

The Princeton Tigers were undefeated and national champions again in 1935. They walloped Yale, 38–7.

Fritz Crisler remained at Princeton until 1938, when he went to the University of Michigan. In his ten years as coach at Michigan he compiled a 71-16-3 record, culminating in a 10-0 national championship team in 1947 that defeated USC, 49–0, in the Rose Bowl. Crisler then became athletic director. He was an influential member of the rules committee and was elected to the College Football Hall of Fame in 1954. Crisler died August 19, 1982.

On February 1, 1935, the Yale Club of New York City hosted a reception and dinner for the varsity team and coaches. In the afternoon DeAngelis, Train, Rankin, and Hersey visited the Boys' Club, where almost 200 youngsters heard them talk about football and education. That evening, about 250 club members heard Ducky Pond speak of the cooperation given him by the players, athletic director, and coaching staff, which he called the best in the nation. Rudy Vallee, class of '27, entertained, and Prescott Bush led them all in a group songfest. From that time, a photo of the eleven Iron Men has hung in the club. The same photo hangs over the entrance door inside Morey's, the private dining club in New Haven celebrated in song.

The entire Yale coaching staff was invited back in 1935. Despite pleas to sign them all to long-term contracts, they returned without contracts. Jimmy DeAngelis and a first-year law student, a center from Michigan named Gerald Ford, were hired as assistant coaches.

Greasy Neale started sending his quarterbacks questionnaires and quizzes in June for the 1935 season. He wrote Jerry Roscoe, "I want you to be perfect in 1935. However, I still say you are the best in America, but you can do better. . . . A great quarterback in 1934 does not make you a wonder in 1935. Study your attack this summer."

The Bulldogs were 6-3 in '35; there was no miracle against Princeton in the Bowl. Among their victories was a 31–20 upset of Penn after trailing, 20-6, and a 7-6 thriller against Navy, the first time they had met the Middies since 1901. Train and Kelley led the defense with more ferocity and stunning goal-line stands. There were several sixty-minute performances. Jerry Roscoe was an even better passer, punt returner, and safety man than he had been in '34. Kim Whitehead did the kicking.

Greasy Neale remained at Yale until 1941, when he became head coach of the Philadelphia Eagles. During his ten years there, he won NFL championships in 1948 and 1949 and was elected to the Pro Football Hall of Fame in 1969. Neale died November 2, 1973, at the age of eighty-one.

Ducky Pond remained at Yale until 1941. He coached at Bates College before and after serving in the navy.

In the book, *My Greatest Day in Football*, Pond singled out the 1934 Princeton game: "There undoubtedly have been greater heroes in Yale football, but I know what these eleven men accomplished that afternoon will find a permanent niche in all football annals. . . . Nobody will ever take away from me my greatest of days—the day that Yale turned back a hitherto undaunted and unconquered Tiger for what to this day is considered among the most stunning upsets in football history."

Ducky Pond died in 1992.

The Iron Men of Yale became an honored institution. At every homecoming game, when alumni gathered in Coxe Cage, one table was set aside as a gathering place for them. Ten of them—all but Strat Morton—made it to their fortieth reunion in 1974. Then gradually their numbers dwindled. Ten years later Jack Wright had died, and Roscoe and Fuller were unable to attend.

Clare Curtin said, "To walk up through the ramp and into the Yale Bowl for the first time in fifty years at the reunion was unforgettable."

There were five—Kelley, DeAngelis, Scott, Roscoe, and Whitehead at the sixtieth and last reunion.

Strat Morton was a second lieutenant in the Army Air Corps. He was killed when the A-20 he was flying crashed in Columbus, Georgia, in June 1941.

Jack Wright was a lieutenant commander in naval aviation during the war and became a management consultant in New York. Wright died in 1978.

Bob Train was offered a contract with the Detroit Lions but turned it down. A lieutenant commander in the navy, he became president of Bibb Manufacturing Company in Macon, Georgia. Train died in 1988.

Ben Grosscup was awarded a Bronze Star in the navy, then was a sales manager at several companies before becoming president of a soft drink manufacturer and distributor in Pittsburgh. Grosscup died in 1993.

Kim Whitehead was a lieutenant commander in naval aviation during the war, then was connected with several gold- and platinum-mining companies. After fifty years he had arthroscopic surgery on his aching right knee. Whitehead died in 1995.

Stan Fuller worked for Goodyear Tire and Rubber Company and later as a probation officer and court administrator. Fuller died in 1998.

Larry Kelley became the most famous of the eleven. He was a colorful, quotable character who gained a national reputation for wisecracks, most of which were made up by George Trevor of the *New York Sun*. Most—but not all. Part of it might be called the luck of the Irish. Or maybe Kelley made his luck. He always seemed to be in the right place at the right time, coming up with one spectacular play after another.

"If the ball dropped out of the sky," said Meredith Scott, "it would go to Kelley."

As an example, Scott described a kick he had blocked with his face in the 1934 Brown game. "On a blocked kick you try to use your upper arms to protect your face," he said. "They had blocked me and I was pushing through and the ball came off the kicker's foot and went right in my face. Sparks flew and the lights went out. The ball bounced about fifteen feet into the air right into Kelley's hands and he ran it in for the touchdown. When I could see again, we were lining up for the extra point and the headline writers were setting up 'KELLEY SCORES' again."

Scott recalled an incident in the 1936 game against Navy in Baltimore. "We punted and Kelley and I were racing down the field almost stride for stride and the ball bounced off the Navy receiver's chest and hit the ground. Kelley was running fast and the ball connected with his foot at the 25. He kicked it to the 3 where he picked it up and ran it over the goal line. The referee allowed it. At first Kelley claimed he had done it on purpose, but when he found out that was illegal, he said he couldn't help it. It looked to me like he just ran into it."

The officials agreed that it was accidental. They placed the ball at the 3, as the rules prohibited running with a fumble.

Clint Frank ran it in for the winning touchdown in Yale's 12–7 triumph.

In the 31–20 win over Penn, played in Philadelphia, Kelley caught two long passes for touchdowns. Scott said, "A man named Kelly was running for mayor of Philadelphia. Right after Kelley scored, an airplane passed over the field dragging a banner: 'Kelly for Mayor.'"

Elected captain of the 1936 team, Kelley and halfback Clint Frank led Yale to a 7-1 record and a number twelve ranking in the new Associated Press polls. That year Kelley was the second winner of the Heisman Trophy. Clint Frank became the third in 1937.

(A picture of the letter men of the 1935 team hung on the wall of John Hersey's office in Vineyard Haven, Massachusetts. "There were only twenty-two of us . . . and when repairmen—or anyone who knows anything about football—come along and I can say that's me standing there and there are two Heisman Trophy winners in the picture, Kelley and Clint Frank, the latter standing beside me, my stock goes sky high.")

Kelley was drafted by the Detroit Lions of the NFL. They promised to get him a job in Detroit that, with his football pay, would earn him $11,000. He also had offers to go into professional wrestling. He turned them both down. He coached and taught at his old school, Peddie, for five years, worked for a glove manufacturer, then taught and coached at Cheshire Academy before returning to Peddie. Kelley died in 2000.

Jerry Roscoe worked for Pan American Airways, setting up bases for ferrying planes during World War II, had a long career with the company, then became an advertising account executive in New York. Roscoe died in 2003.

Meredith Scott played some pro football in the Dixie League, receiving $50 a week for a Sunday game and two nights' practice. He played against the newly transferred Washington Redskins three times (they didn't have a full schedule after moving from Boston), Pittsburgh, and Brooklyn. Scott played three years with the Richmond Arrows. He was in the naval reserve and stayed in the navy, reaching the rank of commander. Later he was in the insurance business. Scott died in 2004.

Clare Curtin was in the navy, then became a high school English teacher and coach, retiring after thirty-two years at the high school in Needham, Massachusetts. Curtin died in 2007.

Jimmy DeAngelis was an assistant football coach at Yale until he joined the navy in 1942, was head freshman coach 1945–48, then was on coaching staffs at several universities before becoming sales manager for a Buick dealership and later for a concrete pipe company in Hamden, Connecticut. His back, hurt in the first five minutes of the 1934 Penn game, bothered him the rest of his life.

On November 18, 2006—one day after the seventy-second anniversary of the day the Iron Men legend was born, the last survivor, Jimmy DeAngelis, saw his last Yale football game at the Bowl, a 34–13 victory over Harvard. DeAngelis died December 28, 2007, at the age of ninety-seven.